The Heracles of Euripides

The Focus Classical Library
Series Editors • James J. Clauss and Michael R. Halleran

Hesiod's *Theogony* • Richard Caldwell • 1987
The *Heracles* of Euripides • Michael R. Halleran • 1988
Aristophanes' *Lysistrata* • Jeffrey Henderson • 1988
Sophocles' *Oedipus at Colonus* • Mary Whitlock Blundell • 1990
Euripides' *Medea* • Anthony Podlecki • 1991
Aristophanes' *Acharnians* • Jeffrey Henderson • 1992
Aristophanes' *The Clouds* • Jeffrey Henderson • 1993

Also of Interest
Studies in Etymology • Charles W. Dunmore •1993

Copyright © 1988 Michael R. Halleran

ISBN 0-941051-01-3
Library of Congress 87-083735
Revised Printing 1993

Cover Photo: Herakles Strangling the Nemean Lion; Iolaus and Hermes. Attic black-figured amphora, sixth century B.C. (76.41). © 1988, all rights reserved, Museum of Fine Arts, Boston MA. Used with permission.

Distributed in Great Britain and Europe by
Gerald Duckworth and Company Ltd
The Old Piano Factory
48 Hoxton Square
London N1 6PB ENGLAND

This book is published by Focus Information Group, Inc., PO Box 369, Newburyport MA 01950. All rights are reserved. No part of this publication may be reproduced, stored in a retrieval system, produced on stage or otherwise performed, transmitted by any means, electronic, mechanical, by photocopying, recording, or by any other media or means without the prior written permission of the publisher. Printed in the United States of America.

The Heracles of Euripides

Translated with Introduction, Notes, and Interpretative Essay

Michael R. Halleran
University of Washington

Focus Classical Library
Focus Information Group, Inc.
PO Box 369
Newburyport MA 01950

To Erin,
Rebecca and Thomas
With love

Table of Contents

Preface . . . . *vii*
   Map of Euripides' Greece . . . . *x*
Introduction
   Euripides 1
   The *Heracles* in Performance 5
   The Myth 11
The *Heracles* of Euripides 15
The *Heracles*: An Interpretation 71
Suggestions for Further Reading 85

Preface

The *Heracles* of Euripides is an extraordinary play, innovative in its treatment of the myth, bold in its dramatic structure, and filled with affecting human pathos. Heracles was the greatest hero of the Greek world. After completing manifold adventures, after doing battle with beasts, Amazons, and the Giants, and returning even from the underworld, he eventually underwent an apotheosis and joined the gods on Mount Olympus. Euripides focuses on one specific section of this long and variegated myth: Heracles' return from the underworld, the rescue of his family, the subsequent fit of divinely-caused madness, which leads him to kill his wife and children, and the eventual rescue of Heracles by his friend Theseus. The play tells a tale of horror: a man murdering his wife and children. The greatest hero of Greece is brought to the lowest and most pitiful position. Euripides here, as in other plays, most notably in *Hippolytus* and *Bacchae*, raises the issue of divine justice. This madness is sent by the gods; the audience sees Iris and Lyssa arrive to cause the ruin of a seemingly blameless man. But suffering and apparent divine malevolence are not the only striking features of this drama. We also witness the moving friendship of Theseus, who takes great risks to save Heracles.

As was the standard practice for plays of the period, the *Heracles* was written for a single performance at a religious festival and did not have an extended "run". The text of the play was preserved and copies of it were made and sold. Eventually it was collected in a complete edition of Euripides' plays and it survives primarily in a manuscript of the fourteenth century. In the long course of transmission various errors were introduced into the text and the job of the textual critic is to determine as precisely as possible the actual words of the poet. It is fortunate that an excellent text of Euripides' *Heracles* has been produced recently by James Diggle (*Euripidis Fabulae* vol. 2 [Oxford 1981]), on which my translation is based, with only occasional exceptions. The *Heracles* presents in many ways a difficult text. In interpreting it I have benefited not only from Diggle's splendid edition, but from the work of other scholars, most notably the commentary of G. Bond (*Euripides: Heracles* [Oxford 1981]), the text and commentary of Wilamowitz (*Euripides: Herakles*, 2nd ed., 3 vols. [Berlin 1895], and of L. Parmentier and H. Grégoire (*Euripide. Tome 3. Héraclès, Les Suppliantes, Ion* [Paris 1950]). I have also found very useful two extensive reviews of Bond's work: D. Mastronarde, "Review Article: Euripides' *Heracles*," *Echos du Monde Classique/Classical Views* 2 (1983) 93-116, and R. Renehan, "Review Article: A New Commentary on Euripides," *Classical Philology* 80 (1985) 143-75.

Translation is the carrying across of expressions and ideas from one language to another. Of the many aspects of language not all can be conveyed at once successfully. Ultimately translation is a type of interpretation, and there are almost as many styles of interpretation as there are interpreters. In translating the *Heracles* I have attempted to be true to its expression and structure. To the extent that it is possible I have followed the colometry of the Greek text and have done little to alter the idioms and metaphors of the original, trying to preserve the movement as well as the texture of the poetry. I have made no attempt to reproduce the rhythm of the verse of the dialogue (a six-beat iambic line, called the iambic trimeter) or of the lyrics. In translating the lyric sections closely, I have found that they maintain some of their lyric quality. In short, I have tried to present Euripides' play to the reader accurately and with as few barriers as possible.

A number of lines found in the manuscripts are not, in all probability, originally by Euripides but are the result of interpolation. These lines are translated here and are indicated by square brackets.

There are basically two systems for transliterating Greek proper names, one which reproduces transliterations directly from the Greek, another, the traditional one, which derives the English spellings from the Latinized forms of the names. I have opted for the traditional spellings.

The *Heracles* not only was written in a different language but was part of a different culture, whose shared beliefs, customs, and symbols are often unfamiliar to us. In writing the notes I have intended to bridge this cultural gap. The identities of persons and places have been given, as have explanations of customs or ideas which were clear to the original audience but confusing or opaque to us. I have tried to let the translation "speak for itself" and accordingly have used the notes only occasionally to annotate the nuance of a word or phrase. Since no stage directions accompany the ancient text, stage actions must be inferred from the play itself and from an understanding of the conventions of the ancient Greek theater. I have indicated only those actions which seem clear from the text, although doubtless there were others in the original performance. Stage directions are indicated in italics in the text and at times elaborated in the notes.

The introduction has three sections, offering sketches of Euripides and his age, the circumstances of the original production, and the background of the myth. An interpretative essay follows the work itself. Suggestions for further reading will be found at the end of the book.

My interest in the *Heracles* is of long standing, and I am pleased to have had the opportunity to produce this translation with notes, introduction and essay. I am also pleased to have the chance to express my gratitude to those who aided me in my work. First, I would like to acknowledge the support and encouragement I received from the Classics Department and my colleagues at the University of Washington. Particularly I wish to thank my colleagues Mary Whitlock Blundell and James J. Clauss for reading the manuscript and making numerous useful suggestions. My greatest debt, as always, is owed to my wife Erin. She discussed with me all aspects of the play and this project and read the entire manuscript, improving it with her fine ear and good sense. Above all she has encouraged and sustained me in my endeavor. To Erin and to Rebecca and Thomas this work is lovingly dedicated.

University of Washington
Seattle

In this revised editon I have corrected typographical and other errors and made a few dozen changes. My thanks to Mary Whitlock Blundell (again) and Terence McKiernan for bringing some of the errors to my attention.

Seattle
September 1992

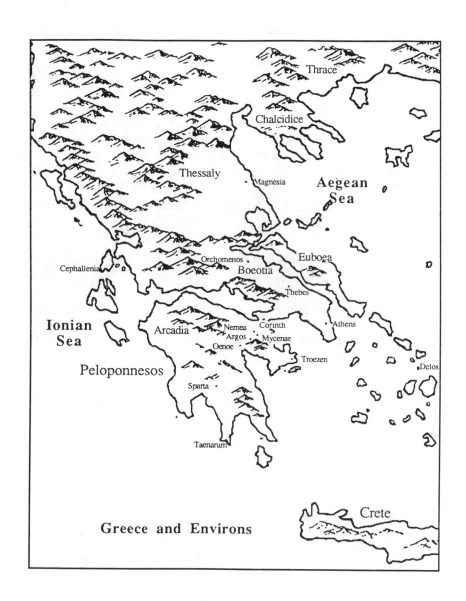

Thrace

Chalcidice

Thessaly

Magnesia

Aegean
Sea

Orchomenos

Euboea

Cephallenia

Boeotia

Thebes

Ionian
Sea

Arcadia

Nemea

Corinth

Athens

Argos

Mycenae

Oenoe

Peloponnesos

Troezen

Delos

Sparta

Taenarum

Crete

Greece and Environs

Introduction

Euripides

Euripides' life spanned most of the fifth century B.C. He was born in the latter part of the 480s (ancient sources record both 485/4 and 480 as dates for his birth) and died in 406. He was an Athenian. His father, named Mnesarchos or Mnesarchides, and his mother Cleito were from the Attic deme Phyla. It seems as if the family was reasonably well off and Euripides himself perhaps rich. Nothing reliable is known of his youth, but it is safe to assume that he received a traditional education, being schooled in letters, music and athletics. In 455 he produced his first plays, the title of one of which we know, the *Peliades* ("daughters of Pelias"). At this time Aeschylus, the most renowned playwright of the early years of the century had just died (in 456) and Sophocles (ca. 496-406/5), was already well established as a tragic poet. Euripides did not win first prize at the festival that year and had to wait until 441 before he took that honor. In fact, Euripides, although very often awarded the honor of putting on plays at the Athenian dramatic festivals, was victorious only four times in his career, and once posthumously. He composed about ninety plays, and on occasion he also wrote in other genres. Near the end of his life he left Athens and moved up north to the court of Archelaos, king of Macedonia, and there he died.

As in the case of all ancient Greek poets, we have little information about Euripides, and much of this is not very reliable. In addition to the information given in the brief sketch above, ancient sources preserve many anecdotes about the poet. Many of these stories, however, are of dubious historical validity; often the plays themselves and the traditions of contemporary comedy are the source for these tidbits about the personal traits and habits of the poet. But although there is much fiction in the biographical tradition, too skeptical an approach is unwarranted. From the ancient traditions and their half-truths a certain picture of the poet begins to emerge, even if the details are blurred. Euripides is said to have owned a library, and this in an age of few books. It is reported also that he had a cave on Salamis where he could avoid the crowd and that he was often lost in thought. The stories about Sophocles, themselves exaggerated and even apocryphal, suggest an ideal citizen, active in the social, religious, and military life of Athens. This picture of Sophocles and the contrasting one of Euripides were very possibly drawn in caricature in order to highlight the differences between the two men, but it seems unlikely that the differences were invented from whole cloth. The ancient sources seem to suggest that Euripides was something of a loner (although we need not assume a misanthrope), who was more caught up than his contemporaries in the intellectual movements of his age.

Athens was experiencing its most exciting and stimulating era. In fact, Euripides' life is virtually framed by the rise and fall of Athenian pre-eminence. The year 480 is given as one of the dates for his birth perhaps because of the ancient predilection for linking together important events, in this case the birth of the poet Euripides and the battle of Salamis. At this battle the Greek navy defeated the Persians, and, although hostilities between the two powers continued, this signaled an end to the threat of Persian attempt to dominate Greece. The victory not only freed Greece from the decades-old threat of Persian rule but helped to establish the dominant role of Athens in Greek affairs, for it was the Athenian naval initiative, led by Themistocles, which drove back the Persians. What this victory over the Persians guaranteed and what the Athenians valued so dearly was freedom. Athens had recently cast off its own tyrants and was ruled by a democracy, which became even more democratic as the century progressed. There continued to be supporters of oligarchy in Athens, but they did not hold sway. An important consequence of the prominent role of Athens in the Persian defeat was the great confidence it inspired, confidence which strengthened and characterized the city-state for most of the century. Freedom of speech was part of this confidence and of Athenian democracy. Thought of by Athenians as their privilege, this freedom helped create the environment hospitable to the great intellectual achievements of this age. In some ways Athens remained a conservative community, and trials for impiety (the most famous being that of Socrates in 399) are recorded. But Euripides, Sophocles, the comic poet Aristophanes (ca. 445- ca. 385) and others worked in a city which permitted and in no small part fostered their genius. It is difficult to imagine the *Heracles* being written and produced in the more constricting environment of Sparta or Corinth.

Over the next fifty years after the defeat of the Persians Athens would become the most powerful city-state in the Greek world and, perhaps inevitably, the most ambitious and feared. This so-called "golden age" of Athens came to an end when Sparta, the other leading city-state of the Greek world, and her allies went to war with Athens and her allies, in the Peloponnesian War. As the contemporary historian Thucydides wrote in his account of the war (1.23), "I consider that the truest cause [of the war], although most concealed officially, was that the Athenians, by becoming powerful and causing fear to the Spartans, compelled them to war." Hostilities had flared before between these two powers earlier in the century, but this war was on a much greater scale. With some interruptions the war went on from 431 until the defeat of Athens in 404, shortly after Euripides' death.

However shortlived Athens' dominance would prove to be, its accomplishments during this period can not be ignored. Like Paris and New York in later ages, Athens was the center of artistic and intellectual activity for the Greek world, producing and attracting the leading practitioners of the various arts. The confidence and political leadership following the Persian Wars contributed to this in no small measure. Under the leadership of Pericles, an extraordinary building program was undertaken on the acropolis, culminating in the erection of the magnificent temple to Athena, the Parthenon, which showed off Athenian excellence in architecture and sculpture. (This and other ambitious projects were aided by money collected from the so-called Delian league, which was formed originally as an alliance against the Persian threat but was eventually based in and exploited by Athens.) Vase painting, depicting domestic and mythological scenes alike, reached its acme in this period and had its finest workshops in Athens. Athens was also the "home" for tragedy and comedy, the two most important literary genres of the age.

Very important for Euripides' career was the contemporary intellectual movement, named after a group of men collectively referred to as the sophists. This group of men, Protagoras, Anaxagoras, and Prodicus among them, did not constitute a "school" but were individuals who toured Greece and in many instances resided in Athens for long periods. They were teachers, offering instruction in a wide variety of topics, from astronomy to rhetoric. Much of their teaching was aimed at practical knowledge which would help their students be successful at whatever they did. Rhetoric played a large a role in their instruction in part because in a democracy the ability to speak well and sway public opinion, whether in the law court or the assembly, was crucial for success. But some of their teaching was in more theoretical areas such as epistemology and theology. Some idea of the sophists' intellectual concerns may be gleaned from a few quotations. Protagoras wrote, "About the gods, I am not able to know whether they exist or not nor what form they have. For many things impede this knowledge, the obscurity [of the issue] and the shortness of a human's life" (frag. 4). And, again, "Of all things a man is the measure, of those that are, that they are, and of those that are not, that they are not" (frag. 1). These fragments give a brief glimpse of the fundamental nature of some of the sophists' inquiries. And man is placed at the center of the inquiry. We can also see their keen interest in rhetoric in a statement made by another sophist, Gorgias: "Speech is a great ruler, which with the smallest and least manifest body accomplishes divine deeds" (*Helen* 8).

Euripides is linked to these thinkers in the biographical tradition: the three men mentioned above were said to have been his teachers (the biographers' was of saying "there is a connection between"), and Socrates is recorded as his friend. Also his plays reflect the influence of these and other contemporary thinkers. Euripides was not the only playwright to be influenced by these contemporary thinkers: Sophocles and the author of *Prometheus Bound*, for example, also can be seen responding to the ideas and questions of these men. But Euripides, the ancient biographies reported, and his plays seem to reveal, was more influenced by them. Or perhaps it is more accurate to say that he was more concerned with the issues with which they too were concerned. Rhetoric, at times self-conscious, is more prominent in his plays than in those of Aeschylus and Sophocles. And questions of the gods and divine justice are at the forefront of several of his plays, as we see, for example in *Heracles*, *Hippolytus*, and *Bacchae*. Stories of Euripides being charged with impiety may well be apocryphal, but they reflect the discomfort which some Athenians may have felt at his frequently disturbing plays.

Although only mildly successful in his own time, Euripides' works became very popular after his death, in part because his interests prefigured those of later ages. (In fact, Euripides is often thought of as the most modern of the three tragedians.) His plays were frequently performed and their texts often reproduced. Owing to his later popularity and a stroke of good fortune, many more plays of Euripides survive than of Sophocles or Aeschylus. Eighteen genuine plays (plus the probably spurious *Rhesus*) are found in the manuscripts, the oldest one of which containing all these plays dates from the early fourteenth century. We have, in other words, almost a full fifth of the poet's total dramatic output, compared with, for example, about six percent of Sophocles' plays. Ten of these plays (including the *Rhesus*) derive from the gradual process of selection, a process which took place also for Aeschylus and Sophocles, which culminated in these ten in about 200 A.D.; these are the often called the "select plays". The other plays survive by chance from what was once a complete edition of Euripides; the *Heracles* is one of these plays. Thus we have plays of Euripides which were not subject to the tastes and decision making of later antiquity. Since these all come from the same section of the alphabet, they are called the "alphabetic plays". In addition to these plays which are preserved in full, many fragments from other plays survive (more than in the case of the other two tragedians).Often of considerable size, these fragments, in conjunction with *hypotheseis*, ancient plot summaries, and other information, allow for a reconstruction of the plays. In short, we have a fuller picture of Euripides' dramatic work than we have of that of either Aeschylus or Sophocles.

This fuller picture does not permit a monolithic view of the playwright. Several of his plays, for example, often called the "romances" (*Helen, Ion,* and the *Iphigenia among the Taurians*) have "happy endings" and do not conform to a strict notion of tragedy. Other plays have unusual structures and twists, while others offer very novel treatment of the mythological material. The many Euripidean plays that survive suggest a very diverse, clever and thoughtful playwright. If he is harder to pin down as a result, he is all the more stimulating and fascinating. And we should be careful not to isolate the "intellectual" side of his dramas, as if it could be divorced form the plays themselves: Euripides was a dramatist, writing plays that were meant to be performed and most fully understood in performance.

The *Heracles* in Performance

The *Heracles* was first performed in the latter part of the fifth century B.C. (probably within a year or two of 415), in Athens at an annual religious festival. The day it was performed, some 15,000 people, mainly Athenians, gathered together in the large, open-air theater of Dionysus, which was located in the god's precinct and adjacent to his temple on the southern slope of the acropolis, to view the plays to be performed that day. The *Heracles* was a play called a *tragoidia*, a tragedy, or more generally a *drama*. *Drama* etymologically means "the thing done, enacted". Yet our direct experience is with the written word, and even this is tenuous, as the earliest manuscript which preserves this play dates from the fourteenth century. Moreover the play in this (and other) manuscripts is removed from its context, and it offers no explicit stage directions or information about the music and dance that were part of the performance. The words themselves are vivid, moving and finely-textured poetry, but we must remember that they were part of a larger structure of words and action. Fortunately, the plays themselves, while containing no explicit information about production, provide much evidence from which to make inferences and to establish the patterns and conventions of the ancient Greek theater. There are also two other rich sources of information: writers in later antiquity provided anecdotes and material which can be mined and sifted for useful gems, and the archaeological record, including, of course, the remains of the theaters themselves, tells us a great deal about the physical circumstances of performance.

The theater of Dionysus was large. At the time of Lycurgus (latter part of the fourth century B.C.) it could seat by modern estimates approximately 15,000 spectators. Built on the southern slope of the acropolis, its rows of seats went up the hill. The viewing area was called the *theatron,* whence English "theater"; the performance itself took place below. The *orchestra,* a spacious circular dancing area, dominated the spectator's view. About sixty-five feet in diameter, it was the chief area of activity during the play. The other main focus of attention was the *skene,* an (originally) located wooden building, with a roof strong enough to support more than one actor, at the far side of the *orchestra.* It served as the backdrop for the play's action, being the palace at Thebes, as in *Heracles,* or whatever the world of the play claimed. Some scene painting was employed, but our knowledge of this aspect of the original productions is meager. In addition to providing the backdrop for the drama's action, the *skene* also was a stage building, a changing room. The building also helped in projecting the actors' voices in the large open-air theater. How many doors the *skene* had in this period remains a debated question. It obviously had at least one, and it very possibly had two or three. Certainly some scenes in some plays would have been much easier to stage if we assume more than one door was available for comings and goings.

The *skene* offered one place from which characters in the play could enter and to which they could exit. But characters could also enter into the *orchestra* and leave it along the two long entrance ramps, each one commonly called a *parodos,* which led at angles on either side into the acting area. Most of the entrances and exits in a Greek tragedy occurred along these long ramps. It is important to remember in this regard the great openness of the Greek theater: "The dramatic weight of comings and goings is proportional to the openness of space that the Greek theater presented to the playwright, who was also the producer, for exploitation."[1]

Characters in the dramas usually entered and exited on the ground, but could also appear on high. A crane-like device called the *mechane* was available, very likely by the time of the *Heracles,* for divine appearances aloft. The roof of the skene could also be used for divine appearances as well as for mortals' activities. The *ekkyklema* is another device whose existence, although certain for later periods in the theater, is doubted by some for the fifth-century. The *ekkyklema* was a platform which could be rolled out into the acting area and

---

[1] J. Gould, "Tragedy in Performance," in *The Cambridge History of Classical Literature,* vol. 1 *Greek Literature,* eds. P. Easterling and B. Knox (Cambridge 1985) 270.

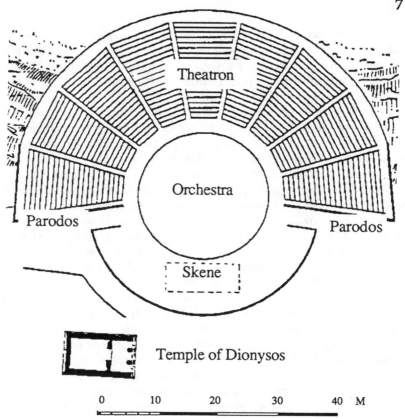

Temple of Dionysos

0   10   20   30   40 M

A reconstruction of the theater of Dionysus in Athens during Euripides'
career, the second half of the fifth century B.C. (Based on the sketch by
J. Travlos, *Pictorial Dictionary of Ancient Athens* [London 1971] 540).

permitted an interior scene to be shown to the audience. One of the
conventions of the Greek stage was that all the action takes place
outdoors, so anything that occurs inside must be revealed to the
audience through voices from off stage, an eye-witness account of the
event, or the scene presented on the *ekkyklema*. (Sometimes, as in the
Heracles, all three methods are employed.) In all probability this
device was used for the original production of the *Heracles* and was a
potential resource for any contemporary tragedian.

Was there at this point in the history of the theater a stage, an
elevated platform in the *orchestra* to be used by the actors, while the
chorus, the other members of the production, operated in the *orchestra*
proper? It *may* be that there was a slightly raised stage as in the
orchestra and used by the actors during this period. Later in the history
of the theater the stage became significantly elevated, furthering the
distance and distinction between the world of the chorus and the

8

world of the actors. This was not the case in the fifth century. As the plays themselves make amply clear, even if the actors are on a slightly raised platform, they and the chorus communicate freely with one another and can impinge on each other's acting area; no barrier is felt between the two groups.

Tragedy was very much a part of the *polis*, the city-state, and had been since the performance of tragedies was first instituted by the *polis* in ca. 534. The plays were put on during a religious festival, the City Dionysia, sponsored by the state in honor of the god Dionysus, and were financially supported by wealthy citizens chosen by a state official. (The playwrights had other opportunities for producing their plays, but the original forum for their productions, the City Dionysia, remained the most prestigious and consistently drew, it seems, the best dramatists.) As the occasion was a religious holiday, work was suspended and a relatively large number of the citizens would attend. The holiday was an annual festival celebrated over several days in the month Elaphebolion (roughly our March). The festival included a torch-light procession, sacrifice, and various artistic competitions (choruses, tragedies and comedies). Although these plays were performed at a religious festival, they were not religious in the sense in which we usually understand the term: they were not necessarily or even frequently about religious dogma or ritual. Although, like so much of Greek literature, they often were in part concerned with questions of the gods' interaction with mortals, these plays honored the gods primarily by their excellence, their display of artistic achievement.

Greek society was agonistic. The plays were put on in competition: three playwrights competed for prizes. Even to be able to compete one had to be selected by the magistrate in charge of the festival, the eponymous archon (the magistrate who gave his name to the Athenian calendar year), who presumably made his selection on the basis of a sample of the playwright's work. In the expression of the Greeks, a playwright, wishing to put on plays at the festival, "asked for a chorus" and the archon "granted a chorus". Each of the three playwrights would produce three tragedies and a satyr play, a type of burlesque, playful tragedy. The same magistrate who selected the three poets to put on plays at the festival also chose three of the city's wealthy citizens to finance most of the expenses incurred in a production. The *choregos*, as each of these three men was called, although he could influence a production's outcome considerably by his generosity or parsimony, was not in charge of the nuts and bolts of production. This duty, or rather duties, fell to the playwright, who was director, usually choreographer, and, originally, though later only occasionally, actor for the plays.

Two groups comprised the performers of a Greek tragedy: actors and chorus. All the participants seem to have worn the same basic outfit: an ankle-length robe or tunic (*chiton*) with an outer garment (*himation*) over it. Footwear in this period was not elaborate, but consisted of a simple thin-soled shoe or boot; and occasionally actors or chorus would appear barefoot. Of course there would be variations in costume within a given production and differences from one production to another. All parts were played by men (compare the *onnagata* roles in Japan's Kabuki theater). This might tax our response as spectators, but for the original audience the playing of female roles by male actors both was conventional and was aided greatly by an important feature of these performances—the wearing of masks. The actors, as well as the members of the chorus, all wore full-face masks. Made in this period probably of reinforced linen, they covered the front of the head and had wigs attached. Although no mask survives from this era, vase painting and the evidence of the plays themselves suggest that in general an attempt was made at realism. (Writing in the second century A.D., Pollux lists twenty-eight different types of mask, but the situation in Euripides' day is not certain.) The basic requirement of the mask was to identify a character in distinction from the other characters in the drama. The use of masks not only allowed this recognition of characters (the old man, the young woman, etc.), it also encouraged a close identification between the actor and the role. The mask, in the words of one critic, "presents, it does not re-present."[1] And, of course, the mask did not permit changes in facial expression, the type of nuance which we, accustomed to close-up shots in cinema, have come to expect. (Such fine touches in any case would have been lost to the great majority of spectators in the vast theater of Dionysus.) The mask with its unchanging expression drew attention, as another critic has put it, "not to the unexpressed thought inside, but to the distant, heroic figures, whose constant ethos it portrays."[2]

Of the two constituent parts of a Greek tragedy the chorus perhaps seems the more distant and difficult for a modern audience to appreciate. The members of the chorus, fifteen in number when the *Heracles* was produced, acted usually as a group, singing and dancing their part, a continuous presence in the *orchestra* once they entered. (Their number included a chorus leader, *coryphaeus*, who would at times act independently of the larger group.) This is not what we are used to in modern drama. Music and dance were integral features of the choral elements of the drama. (In fact the Greek word *choros* has "dance" as its primary meaning.) Music from a reed instrument, the

[1] J. Jones, *On Aristotle and Greek Tragedy* (Oxford 1962) 59.
[2] O. Taplin, *Greek Tragedy in Action* (Berkeley and Los Angeles 1978) 14.

aulos, accompanied the performance of the dancing, but the precise nature of the music and of the dancing is impossible to determine from the ancient evidence, although we do know that in general Greek dancing was mimetic.

Even with little information about the music and dance, it is readily apparent that the choral lyrics are rich poetry and important to the drama. All parts of a Greek drama, both the dialogue and the songs, were composed in verse, but the poetry of the songs was different in kind: denser, more striking in its imagery and more suggestive in its language. The chorus has over the years been called the "ideal spectator" and the "voice of the poet". Neither is true. Although the chorus is generally less well defined and at times less integral to the action than the other characters in the play, it does have a specific personality (in our play the old Theban men well-disposed to Heracles and his family) and a definite role to play in the drama. The chorus responds to the action, reflecting on the events and often referring to past events as a context for the current ones. Owing to the nature of their poetry and their function, the choral songs are heard in, as it were, a different key. The typical choral song is strophic, that is to say it is written in paired stanzas, each member of the pair having the same metrical composition. The first member is called the strophe and the second the antistrophe. While the two members of the pair of stanzas are identical rhythmically, no two pairs are alike. After one, two, three or even more paired stanzas, the ode may conclude with a single stanza with no responding element; this is called an epode. The first song is called the *parodos*, the song delivered as the chorus entered into the *orchestra*; subsequent ones are each called a *stasimon*, a song delivered after the chorus had taken up their position in the *orchestra*.

The origins of tragedy remain obscure, but without sailing the murky and shoal-ridden waters of its origins, it is fair to say that tragedy originated as a song sung at a ritual. The name Thespis is attached to the first actor, and this man is often called the creator of tragedy. The stories about this shadowy figure give varied and at times conflicting reports, yet they point to the same essential fact of his profound influence on the history of Western theater: at a time of thoroughly choral presentations, Thespis was the first to break away from the chorus and give speeches and respond to the chorus. With Thespis tragedy ceased to be only a sung narrative and became enriched with a new dimension, that of actors and their *spoken* words. After Thespis introduced the first actor, others were later added: Aeschylus is said to have introduced the second actor and Sophocles the third. There the number of actors with speaking parts became fixed: each dramatist worked with only three actors. Of course a play could have more than three characters, but this would be handled by the "doubling" of roles: one actor would play more than one part. There were so called "mute characters", "extras" who would have silent parts to play, such as attendants and children. The reason for this limit was perhaps aesthetic, perhaps it suggests an attempt at fairness so that all playwrights would be competing for the prizes under the same conditions. Whatever the reason, the effect is noteworthy: the Greek tragic stage, with the exception of the chorus, tended to be rather uncrowded. Dialogue among three characters, although possible, was in fact uncommon. The plays generally show conversations between two characters, or one character and the chorus, or one delivering a soliloquy. Even when the three actors with speaking parts are on stage together, they only infrequently carry on a three-way dialogue. The doubling of roles necessitated by the relatively small number of actors was also facilitated by the masks and the identification they created between the mask-wearing actor and the character he played. In a given drama an actor might play several roles, and with each mask that he donned he became that character and the audience could thereby readily make the adjustment.

As Aristotle long ago observed, the fundamental structure of tragedy is based on the alternation of speech and song, the dialogue of the actors and the songs of the chorus. Periodically in the play the chorus leader will have a few lines to speak, and the actors will occasionally sing their lines, but the basic dynamic of the genre is the alternation of speech and song. This alternation gives tragedy much of its rich and varied texture. Tragedy's structure also involves, as has been more recently demonstrated, not only the alternation of speech and song but this alternation tied up with exits before the song and entrances after them. One should be alert to this basic pattern and variations on it. In particular, since these junctures of song and exit and entrance represent the joints, as it were, of the dramas, one should pay attention to the ways in which the playwright exploits these junctures for significant juxtapositions as he moves in and out of scenes and between the two constituent parts of the drama, actors and chorus, action and song.

The Myth

With uncommon exceptions, the Greek tragedians took the subjects for their plays from the vast reservoir of traditional tales, the myths. By the time of Euripides this included not only orally transmitted tales but also the literary accounts found in epic poets, including of Homer and Hesiod, who composed near the end of the eight century B.C., in lyric poets, such as Stesichorus (late seventh to mid-sixth century) and Pindar (ca. 520- mid-fifth century) and in other

tragedians. Since the poets and playwrights worked with this traditional body of material, it is sometimes erroneously ssumed that the
artist had little freedom, that he simply wrote what had happened
according to myth. But although the playwrights and other poets
worked within a long tradition, they still had a great deal of flexibility
in composing their works. And Greeks myths themselves were rarely
monolithic: there was often more than one version of a story, even if
one rendering had become standard. In choosing from the rich store
of mythological material the playwright made many decisions. The
tradition did place some constraints on the playwright, as certain
events had to occur or be assumed in any account of a given story.
(For example, Oedipus must always murder his father and sleep with
his mother: these facts are essential to the Oedipus myth. Yet even in
this tale, it is noteworthy how Sophocles in his *Oedipus the King*
focuses not so much on these crimes but on Oedipus' discovery of
them and of his own identity.) But it was the playwright who interpreted the myth and gave it his particular view and treatment.

One of the playwright's greatest freedoms in his interpretation
was his freedom of selection. He decided where to begin his tale,
where to end it, which events to include, which to emphasize, which
to downplay. He could reshape the tale in many ways, altering it for
his own dramatic purposes, relying on unfamiliar versions of the tale
and even innovating in certain details. The traditional material, far
from confining the talents of the poet, provided him with the building
blocks of his story and offered him a backdrop by which his account
of the tale would be enriched and against which it would, at least
implicitly, be measured. As a corollary to the poet's freedom in
reshaping the traditional stories, the audience did not know what was
going to happen in the play it was watching. The audience could still
feel suspense, and in fact knowledge of the tradition might add to the
suspense, as the viewer would wonder how or if some feature of the
story would be treated.

Stories about Heracles were many and varied, attesting to his great
importance and popularity in Greek culture. It will be useful to
summarize the basic facts of his myths. Heracles was the child of the
chief Olympian, the sky god, Zeus, and a mortal woman, Alcmene,
the wife of Amphitryon. Hera, Zeus' wife, was outraged at this
adultery and persecuted Heracles even before he was born. On the
day Heracles was due to come into the world, Hera tricked Zeus into
proclaiming that one born of his blood on that day would rule over
those around him (cf. Homer, *Iliad* 19.95ff.). Zeus meant Heracles, but
Hera bought it about that Eurystheus, Zeus' great-grandson, was
born that day (prematurely) and thus from Tiryns could lord it over
Heracles in nearby Thebes. Heracles' persecution at the hands of Hera

and his subservience to Eurystheus are two of the major features of his stories. He is forced to undertake various tasks, eventually canonized as his "twelve labors", at Eurystheus' orders. These adventures provide much of the material for the Heracles myth since they bring him into contact with various peoples and places throughout the Greek world. These exploits, which have many peripheral ones, show Heracles subduing wild creatures, capturing miraculous objects, and even going to and returning from the underworld. Heracles also is involved in numerous other events and places independent of the labors. After the completion of his labors, Heracles eventually undergoes an apotheosis and becomes a full-fledged Olympian god.

Our sources for Heracles' myths are disparate: some are archaic epic poetry from the eighth century B.C., others are passing references in authors a thousand years later. The pre-Euripidean tradition, i.e. what Euripides had to work with and what he would assume his audience knew, is difficult to determine with precision. (Often relatively late sources reveal what seems to be a much earlier version of a tale, so even these accounts are important for this purpose.) But an attempt can be made to reconstruct the pre-Euripidean tradition of the aspects of the Heracles myth most relevant to Euripides' play.

In viewing the *Heracles* the audience would have recognized several familiar features of the story and have been struck by some innovations. There was no playbill handed out in the theater of Dionyus, so the audience would learn the background information in the drama itself, typically in the opening scene. Amphitryon, who delivers the prologue speech, first relates some historical and genealogical information, including his own exile from his native Argos because of his unintentional murder of his wife's father, Electryon. He then explains that Heracles is in Hades, finishing the last of his labors, while a man named Lycus has staged a coup and now threatens Heracles' family with death. The most striking departure from the pre-existing tradition is the sequence of events. According to a likely reconstruction of this earlier version, the murder of the children *preceded* the labors and may have provided the motivation for them, as Heracles performed these deeds in service to Eurystheus as purification for the murders. In Euripides' version, the murders follow the labors; thus the hero is struck with madness and commits the murders at the moment of his greatest triumph, his completion of the labors and return from Hades. Euripides' account of the story also necessitates a different motivation for the labors. Amphitryon explains (17-21) that since he himself is in exile from his native Argos, Heracles acts to "ease [these] misfortunes" as well as to win his own return to his fatherland. Filial piety has replaced purification for kindred murder. The audience would be unsurprised to hear Amphitryon add that this "great price for the return" is paid to Eurystheus, Heracles' mortal persecutor, and that Hera is also involved in causing his labors, since these two, as we have seen, were very much part of the tradition. Theseus' later appearance and his involvement in this stage of the story must also be novel, since the involvement hinges on his rescue by Heracles from the underworld, i.e. during the completion of his labors. Amphitryon's speech introduces one other new element: Lycus and his usurpation of power and his threat to the family. This Lycus, it seems, is a Euripidean invention and found nowhere in Greek literature before this play and nowhere afterwards independent of the play's influence. This new character is of obvious importance for the threat he poses to the family, since this motivates the first section of the play.

An interesting question, which cannot be answered with any certitude, suggests itself: did the audience, aware of the apparent shift in the traditional sequence of events, know or suspect that Heracles at some point in the play would kill his children? What did they think would be the consequences of Euripides' innovation? Some might have suspected or wondered about the possibility of the children's murder, but at the point of Heracles' return Euripides stresses the success of Heracles' homecoming and his subsequent victory over Lycus. If the audience did think at all of the gruesome possibility of the children's murder, that added a finer dimension to the experience of viewing the play, as it would create a tension between what the play suggests and what the viewer fears.

The Heracles of Euripides

CHARA CTERS

AMPHITRYON, Heracles' mortal father
MEGARA, Heracles' wife
CHORUS of Theban elders
LYCUS, usurper of power in Thebes
HERACLES
IRIS, messenger of the gods
LYSSA, Madness personified
MESSENGER
THESEUS, king of Athens
HERACLES' AND MEGARA'S THREE SONS
LYCUS' ATTENDANTS

Setting: Outside the palace of Heracles in Thebes, Amphitryon, Megara, and her three sons by Heracles sit as suppliants on the steps of the altar of Zeus Soter (Zeus the Rescuer), seeking to escape death at the hands of Lycus, the recent usurper in Thebes. In typical Euripidean fashion, the play begins with a speech which conveys the basic background information to the audience and helps to establish the play's mood.

Amphitryon
What mortal does not know of the man who shared his marriage
    bed with Zeus,
Amphitryon of Argos,[1] whom Alcaeus, Perseus' son,
Once begot, me, the father of Heracles?
I took Thebes here as my home, where the earth-born
Crop of Spartoi[2] grew up, whose race Ares[3]   5

---

[1] Argos was an important city in the eastern Peloponnese (see map).

[2] Cadmus, the legendary founder of Thebes, killed a serpent and, following the goddess Athena's advice, sowed half of its teeth. From these teeth sprouted up the Spartoi (the "sown men"), who fought one another (incited, according to some accounts, by Cadmus throwing a rock among them) until only five remained. The prominent families of Thebes claimed to be descended from these. They should not be confused with the Spartans, inhabitants of Sparta.

[3] Ares, the Greek god of war, is perhaps used here metaphorically for battle, but he was the father of the serpent whose teeth were sown.

Saved in small number, and these populated the city of Cadmus
With their children's children. From these came
Menoeceus' son Creon, a ruler of this land.
Creon was the father of Megara here,
Whom all the Cadmeans[1] once celebrated   10
With flute and song, when the famous Heracles
Led her as wife to my house.
But my son, leaving behind Thebes, where I had resettled,
Megara and his in-laws,
Was eager to dwell in the Argive fortifications,   15
The Cyclopean city,[2] from which I'm in exile since I killed
Electryon.[3] And trying to ease my misfortunes
And wishing to dwell in his fatherland,
He pays to Eurystheus[4] a great price for the return—
Taming the earth—whether subdued by Hera   20
And her goads or by necessity.
And he's finished toiling with the other labors,
But for the last one he's gone through the mouth of Taenarum[5]
To Hades, so he might bring back to the light
The three-bodied dog;[6] and from there he has not returned.   25
There is an old story among the Cadmeans
That there used to be a certain Lycus, Dirce's husband,
Who ruled this seven-gated city[7]
Before the white-horse ones, Amphion and Zethus,[8]
Offspring of Zeus, became the rulers of the land.   30

---

[1]The Cadmeans, taking their name from Cadmus, were the early inhabitants of Thebes; in this play and elsewhere the name is used virtually as a synonym for "Thebans".

[2]"The Cyclopean city" refers to Mycenae (see map) with its famous fortifications, the city in the Peloponnese which gave its name to the Bronze Age culture of the Greeks. Here and elsewhere in Greek tragedy, Mycenae and Argos are used interchangeably to refer to the same place, in part because of their geographical proximity.

[3]Amphityron unintentionally killed Electryon, Alcmene's father. Blood-guilt commonly provides a motive for exile in Greek myths.

[4]Eurystheus was Heracles' mortal persecutor. The two were cousins: Electryon, Alcmene's father, was half-brother of Eurystheus' father, Sthenelus.

[5]Taenarum was a cape in the southernmost Peloponnese (see map), thought to be an entrance to the underworld, Hades.

[6]The three-bodied dog was Cerberus, the watchdog of the underworld. Capturing him was Heracles' final labor.

[7]Thebes was often referred to by its most salient feature, its seven gates.

[8]Amphion and Zethus, sons of Zeus and the mortal Antiope were in many accounts the founders of Thebes. The precise significance of the epithet "whitehorse ones" is uncertain.

His son, named after his father with the same name,
Not a native Cadmean, but coming from Euboea,[1]
Killed Creon and having killed him rules the land,
After falling upon this city sick with faction.
And for us the marriage bond to Creon   35
Turns out to be, it seems, the greatest ill.
With my son in the chambers of the earth
This new ruler of this land, Lycus,
Wishes to do away with Heracles' children,
Killing them and his wife, so he can quench bloodshed with
    bloodshed,   40
And me (if one may reckon even me, a worthless old man,
Among men), lest these children someday reach manhood
And exact payment for the blood of their mother's kin.
But I (for my child, when he departed for the dark gloom
Of earth, left me behind in this house   45
As a housekeeping nurse for the children)—
To prevent Heracles' children's death, I, along with their mother,
Sit at this altar of Zeus Soter,[2]
Which my noble offspring set up as a dedication
For his victory in war after his defeat of the Minyans.[3]   50
And we keep these positions, lacking everything—
Food, drink, clothing—lying on
The ground without bedding. For locked out
Of the house, we sit here in need of rescue.
Some of our friends I realize are not reliable friends,   55
While others who truly are cannot help.
Such is misfortune for mortals:
May no one who is even moderately friendly to me
Ever meet with it! It is the surest test of friends.

Megara
Old man, who once destroyed the city of the Taphians[4]   60
When you gloriously commanded the army of Cadmeans,
How nothing of the divine is clear for mortals!
I, for instance, on my father's side was not excluded from good
    fortune:

---

[1]Euboea is a large island off the eastern coast of the northern portion of Greece
(see map).
[2]Taking shelter at an altar was supposed to offer protection to the suppliants.
Soter ("Rescuer") was one of Zeus' many cult titles.
[3]Heracles led the Thebans in a victorious batle against the Minyans, inhabitants of northern Boeotia, whose principle city was Orchomenus (see map).
[4]The Taphians were a people located in the Taphian islands and Cephallenia
near the Acarnanian coast in northwestern Greece (see map). Amphitryon
led one of the groups which joined forces in defeating them.

He once was celebrated as great because of his prosperity,
Since he held power, for the love of which   65
Long spears leap against successful men,
And he had children. And me he gave to your son,
Joining me to Heracles in a splendid union.
But now all these things have died and flown away.
And you and I are about to die, old man,   70
Along with Heracles' children, whom I protect
Like a bird with her chicks crouched beneath her wings.
And one after another of them falls to questioning:
"Mother," they say, "Where in the world has he gone to?
What is he doing? When will he return?" Fooled by their
    youth   75
They seek their father, but I put them off,
Telling them tales. And they are all alarmed
Whenever the door creaks, and leap up
As if to fall at their father's knee in greeting.
So now, old man, what hope or means of rescue   80
Do you have at hand? I look to you.
We could not escape from the land's boundaries in secret
(For the guards at the borders are stronger than we are)
Nor in our friends do we any longer have hope
Of rescue. Whatever plan you have,   85
Speak out. Otherwise death is certain.

Amphitryon
Daughter, it is not very easy to give advice on matters such as
    these
Lightly, with earnestness but without effort.
In our weakness let us prolong the time.

Megara
Do you want some further pain? Or do you so love the light?   90

Amphitryon
Yes, I rejoice in it and love its hopes.

Megara
So do I, but you ought not to think the impossible, old man.

Amphitryon
In delays there are cures for ills.

Megara
But the time between is painful and stings me.

Amphitryon
Be that as it may, daughter, a fair sailing might come   95
From your present ills and mine,

And still my child, your husband, might return.
But be calm and check the flood of the
Children's tears and soothe them with words,
Concealing your deceptions, miserable though they are, with
    tales,   100
For even mortals' misfortunes grow weary,
And blasts of winds are not always strong,
And the fortunate are not fortunate to the end.
For all things stand apart separating from one another.
That man is the best, the one who always   105
Trusts in hopes.[1] It is a bad man who is at a loss.

(The chorus, composed of fifteen old men of Thebes, now enters the orchestra down one of the parodoi, entrance ramps, singing and dancing.)[2]

Chorus
Strophe
To the high-vaulted halls and the old man's
Bed we set forth, pivoting for support
Around our staffs,
Aged singers of lamentations,   110
Like the white bird,[3]
Mere words, the nocturnal semblance
Of night-time dreams,
Feeble, but eager still,
O, children, fatherless children,   115
Old man, and you, wretched mother,
Who lament your husband
In the halls of Hades.
Antistrophe
Let's not grow weary of foot and heavy
In our limbs, like a yoked foal   120
Bearing the weight of
Wheel-drawn baggage

---

[1]Hope was by no means viewed by the Greeks primarily as a good; more often than not it was seen as negative, a sign of weakness or delusion. Here Amphitryon seems to be making a virtue of necessity.

[2]The arrival of the chorus is preceded by no particular preparation or announcement, but the audience was accustomed to the choral entrance early in the play. While being very sympathetic to the family, the chorus emphasizes here in the opening song and later (e.g., 268ff.) their weakness and inability to help them, making the need of another rescuer the more keenly felt. This opening song (*parodos*) is short, having only three stanzas of modest length.

[3]The swan was proverbial for its whiteness, renowned for its singing (especially of its dying song) and associated with Apollo and poets.

Up a steep, rocky cliff.
Grab the hands and garments of anyone
Whose footstep falters and is weak.   125
Old man, escort old man,
Who before now, when young,
At one time held youthful spears, allied
In the toils of his comrades,
And was no disgrace to the most glorious fatherland.   130

Epode
Look how these eyes' Gorgon-gleaming[1]
Flashes are like
Those of their father.
Misfortune is not wanting in the children,
Nor is charm.
Greece, such ones,   135
Such allies you will lack
In losing these.

But look—I see this one coming near the house,
Lycus, the ruler of this land.

(Lycus has entered with attendants from one of the parodoi.)

Lycus:[2]
I will question Heracles' father and his wife,   140
If I may. And I may, since in fact I've become
Your master, ask what I wish.
For how long do you seek to prolong your life?
What hope, what defense do you perceive against death?
Do you believe that their father, who lies dead in Hades,   145
Will come back? Since you must die,
You are bringing on yourselves more grief than you deserve,
You, in putting forth empty boasts throughout Greece
That Zeus shared with you your wife and and was partner in
    your child,
And you that you were called wife of the most excellent man. 150

---

[1] The Gorgons were female monsters, decorated with snakes, who would turn to stone anyone who looked at them. Here, and elsewhere in the play, "Gorgon-gleaming" means something like "fierce-eyed".

[2] Lycus has arrived with attendants (as is clear from 240ff.), played by actors with non-speaking roles, so-called "mute" characters. He delivers at once a speech (*rhesis*) which will function as a foil for Amphitryon's long defense of Heracles. The first half of this scene with the pair of "set" speeches on a topic is called an *agon*, contest. Such contests are particularly characteristic of Euripides, unsurprisingly in light of his interest in the sophists and the importance they placed on rhetoric and debate. (See *Introduction*, 3-4.)

So what is the august deed your husband has accomplished,
If he killed and destroyed a marsh snake[1]
Or the Nemean beast, which he claims, after he subdued it with
    snares,
To have killed by the strangling of his arms?[2]
Relying on these achievements do you try to contend? On ac-
    count of these   155
Heracles' children should not die?
He got his reputation, although he had no courage,
In fighting beasts, and was not brave otherwise,
He who never held a shield in his left hand
Nor came near a spearpoint, but carrying his bow and
    arrows,   160
The most cowardly weapon, was ready for flight.[3]
The test of a man, of his courage, is not bow and arrows
But staying steadfast in the ranks and looking, even face-to-face,
At the swiftly advancing swathe of troops.
My behavior involves not shamelessness, old man   165
But prudence, since I know that I killed
Creon, this woman's father, and hold his throne.
Therefore I don't wish, when these children grow up, to have
    left behind
Avengers against me and pay the penalty for what I did.

Amphitryon
Let Zeus defend Zeus' part of his   170
Son. As for me, Heracles, it's my concern
To reveal in words this man's stupidity
About you, for I will not let someone speak ill of you.
First, then, the unspeakable[4] charges (I consider the accusation

---

[1] With the phrase "marsh snake" Lycus refers to one of Heracles' labors, the killing of the Lernean hydra (see below n. on 421), but does so in language which belittles the accomplishment.

[2] Lycus implies that a similarity between the words snares (*brochois*) and arm (*brachionos*) allows Heracles to claim more than is true about his subduing of the Nemean lion (see below n. on 359).

[3] The attack on Heracles' bravery is meant to dismiss any favor which might be owed to the children of a brave benefactor. The debate between Lycus and Amphitryon on this matter may reflect contemporary tactical arguments, but more importantly it offers an opportunity for Amphitryon to sing the praises of Heracles and to show him as more than a man of brawn. It should also be observed, as is clear from this play and many places in Greek literature and art, that Heracles did not exclusively or even primarily use the bow as his weapon.

[4] Certain accusations (e. g. parricide) were not to be spoken in Athens; to do so could lead to prosecution for slander, unless the accusations could be proven true.

Of cowardice against you, Heracles, among unspeakable
    ones),   175
With the gods as witnesses these I must dismiss from you.
I ask Zeus' thunderbolt and his four-horse chariot,
Where you stood and pierced the creatures of earth,[1]
The Giants, in their sides with your winged shafts,
And then celebrated the victory song with the gods.   180
Those wanton four-legged creatures, the race of Centaurs,[2]
Go to Pholoe and ask them, most evil of kings,
What man they would judge most excellent,
If not my son, who you claim only seems so.
And should you ask Abantid Diphrys,[3] which reared you,   185
It could not praise you, since nowhere
Have you done a noble deed to which your fatherland could
    bear witness.
And you criticize that very clever invention, the archer's equip-
    ment;
Listen now to my side and become wise.
The heavily armored soldier is a slave to his armor: 190
Having only one defense, when he's broken his spearpoint
He is unable to save himself from death.
And if those arrayed in battle with him are cowardly,
He himself is dead because of the cowardice of those near him.
But for anyone who can aim well with the bow   195
This is the single best thing: after shooting thousands of arrows
With others he can save himself from death,
And standing afar he wards off the enemy,
Striking them with unseen arrows as they watch,
Not offering himself to his opponents,   200
But being well on guard. In battle this

---

[1]Here and later (1190-92) reference is made to Heracles' service to the gods
during the so-called Gigantomachy, the Battle of the Giants (against the
gods). The Giants were monsters born to Uranus (the original sky god) and
Earth, after he was castrated by his son Cronus and his blood impregnated
Earth. They waged war against Zeus and the other Oylmpians and were
defeated. The subject was popular in literature and art.

[2]The Centaurs were hybrid creatures, having the torso of a man and the trunk
of a horse, and were generally considered uncivilized. Heracles, when
entertained with wine by the Centaur Pholus at Pholoe in Arcadia (see
map), fought off other Centaurs who were attracted by the wine's scent.

[3]The Abantes were a tribe in Euboea (see above n. on 32), where the mountain
Diphrys was also located. Lycus came to Thebes from Euboea, and thus
Amphitryon by metonymy says that Abantid Diphrys reared Lycus. Heracles has glorious and far-flung witnesses to his achievements, while Lycus
doesn't have the support of his "hometown".

Is especially wise—to hurt your enemies
While saving yourself, without being anchored to chance.
These arguments hold the opposite opinion
From yours concerning these matters.   205
But these children, why do you wish to kill them?
What did they do to you? In one respect I think you're wise,
If, base yourself, you fear the offspring
Of the best. But this is still grievous for us
If we must die because of your cowardice,   210
A fate which you ought to be suffering at our hands, we who are
      your betters,
If Zeus had just thoughts towards us.
But if all you wish is to hold the sceptre of this land unharassed,
Allow us to leave the land as exiles;
And you will do no harm by violence nor suffer violence   215
Whenever the wind of god changes for you.
Ah!
Land of Cadmus (I will come against you now
In flinging my words of reproach),
Is such the protection you give Heracles and his children,
Who by himself did battle with all the Minyans[1]   220
And made Thebes able to see with a free man's sight?
Nor do I praise Greece (and I will never endure being
Silent), finding it most cowardly towards my son,
When it should have come bearing fire, spears, arms
To these young birds, in return for the toils of his hand   225
In cleansing the sea and the earth.
But, children, neither the city of the Thebans
Nor Greece is strong enough for you. And you look to me,
A friend with no strength, nothing except the sound of my voice.
The might we had before is wanting,   230
My limbs tremble with age and my strength is faint.
But if I were young and still master of my body
I would take up a spear and bloody those
Blond locks of his, so that when he saw my spear
He'd flee in cowardice beyond the bounds of Atlas.[2]   235

Chorus leader
      Don't the good among mortals have the resources
      For arguments, even if they're sluggish at speaking?

Lycus
      You, speak ill of me with the words you've exalted yourself with,

---

[1]See above, n. on 50.

[2]Atlas held up the heavens somewhere in the farthest west; the bounds of
  Atlas are the limits of the civilized world.

But I, in return for these words, will do you ill.
Go now, some to Helicon, others to the glens of Parnassus,[1]   240
And order woodsmen to cut down
Trees; and when they are brought into the city,
Pile up the wood, fitting it around the altar,
And kindle and burn them up,
All of them, so that they may learn that not the dead man   245
Rules this land, but I do now.
As for you, old men, since you're opposed to
My views, you will lament not only
The children of Heracles, but also your own house's
Fortunes, when it suffers something, and you'll remember   250
That you are slaves of my rule.

Chorus leader

Children of earth, whom Ares once sowed
After leaving the serpent's grasping jaw desolate,[2]
Will you not lift up your staffs, the supports
Of your right hand, and bloody this man's   255
Impious head, who, not a Cadmean,
But a most base outsider, rules over my people?
But you will never rule over me with impunity
Nor will you have the many things I toiled and labored for
With my hands. Go back where you came here from   260
And show your insolence. As long as I'm alive you will never kill
Heracles' children. Not by that much earth
Is he hidden below, after leaving behind his children.
Since you have destroyed this land,
He who helped it does not obtain what he ought.   265
Am I a busybody then in helping my friend[3]
When he's dead and most needs his friends?
Right hand, how you desire to pick up a spear,
But you lost the desire by your weakness,
Since otherwise I would have stopped you, Lycus, from calling
    me a slave   270

---

[1]Helicon and Parnassus are mountains, the former not far from Thebes, the latter a considerable distance away in Phocis (see map).

[2]See n. on 5 above; the chorus leader is addressing the chorus.

[3]The word translated here as "friend", *philos*, is important in this play (see already Amphitryon at 55ff.) and in Greek culture generally. Although "friend" is its best English equivalent, *philos* had a wider range of meaning in Greek: it included those related by blood or marriage as well as non-family members, referring to anyone who was near and dear. Central to Greek ethics was the principle of helping your friends (*philoi*) and hurting your enemies (*echthroi*), a principle which motivates much of the action of this play.

And we would have lived honorably here in Thebes,
In which you delight. A city does not have good sense
When it's sick with faction and bad counsels;
Otherwise it would never have gotten you as ruler.

Megara

Old men, thank you. On account of friends   275
Friends ought to show just anger.
But in your anger at the ruler on our account
May you suffer no ill. Hear, Amphitryon,
My opinion, if I seem to you to be saying anything.
I love my children. How could I not love   280
Those I bore and for whom I toiled? And death
I consider terrible, but I think whatever mortal
Strives against necessity is stupid.
But we, since we must die, ought to die
Not wasted by fire, giving laughter   285
To our enemies, which to my mind is a greater ill than death.[1]
We owe many fine things to our house:
You got an illustrious reputation for combat
So that it's intolerable for you to die through cowardice,
While my husband needs no witnesses for his glory,   290
And he would be unwilling to save these children
At the price of their getting a bad reputation. For the noble
Are distressed at their children's disgraces;
And I must not thrust away the example of my husband.
Look at how I consider your hope.   295
Do you think that your child will come back from beneath the
        earth?
And who of the dead has come back from Hades?
But maybe we might soften this man with words?
Impossible. One should flee the stupid enemy
And yield to those who are wise and well bred,   300
Since more easily, submitting to their sense of shame, you would
        come to friendly agreement.
Already it's occurred to me that we might obtain
Exile for these children. But this would be miserable,
Investing them with rescue at the cost of wretched poverty,
Since for friends in exile, they say,   305
Hosts have a kindly look for only one day.

---

[1]Greek culture, which has often been called, with some exaggeration, a
"shame culture", placed great importance on the external, public manifes-
tations of excellence and its opposite. Hence the point made here about
being the object of laughter for one's enemies and the importance attached
below (289ff.) to reputation. See above, n. on 266.

Endure death with us, which awaits you in any case.
We call upon your nobility, old man.
Whoever struggles against the fortunes of the gods
Is eager, but his eagerness is senseless.   310
For no one will ever make what must happen not happen.

Chorus Leader

If someone had treated you insolently
When my arms had strength, I would have stopped him easily.
But now I'm nothing. From this point it's up to you to see
How you will break through these bad blows of fortune.   315

Amphitryon

Neither cowardice nor a craving for life
Keeps me from death, but I wish to save
My child's children. But I seem to desire the impossible in vain.

(He leaves the altar.)

Look, this neck is ready for your sword:
Stab me, kill me, throw me from a cliff.   320
But give us two one favor, lord, we ask:
Kill me and this wretched woman before you kill the children,
So that we don't look upon a dreadful sight,
The children breathing their last and calling, "Mother,
Grandfather." But the rest, if you're eager,   325
Accomplish it; for we don't have the might to prevent death.

Megara

I, too, beg you to add a favor to this favor,
So you alone may serve the two of us two-fold:
Open the house (we are locked out)
And let me clothe the children in the adornment of the dead   330
So that this at any rate they can receive from their father's house.

Lycus

This will be done. I command attendants to open the doors.
Go inside and get dressed; I don't begrudge the robes.
But when you've put on your garments
I will come to you to give you to the earth below   335

(Exit Lycus with his attendants down the parodos from which they entered.)

Megara

Children, accompany your wretched mother's step
Into your father's house, where others
Rule over the property, though the name is still ours.

(Exit Megara with the children into the palace.)

Amphitryon
Zeus, in vain I got you as a partner of my wife,
In vain I called you partner in my child.   340
You were after all less of a friend than you seemed.
I, a mortal, defeat you, a great god, in excellence,
For I did not betray Heracles' children.
But you knew how to go secretly into beds,
Taking others' wives when no one offered,   345
But you do not know how to save your friends.
You are some ignorant[1] god or by nature unjust.

(Exit Amphitryon into the palace.)[2]

Chorus:[3]
Strophe a
Phoebus[4] cries woe,
After a song of good fortune,
As he strikes the beautiful-voiced lyre   350
With a golden pick;
And I wish to celebrate in eulogy
As a crown for his labors
The son who went into the gloom of earth
And of the dead—

---

[1]The word translated as "ignorant" (*amathes*) also suggests "unfeeling, insensitive".

[2]The stage in Greek tragedy was in general not very busy, with relatively few entrances and exits, and these rarely occurred in quick succession. Therefore it is striking to find the successive exits of Lycus, Megara with the children, and Amphitryon within twelve lines of each other. (In only one other place in all of Euripides is there anything comparable [*Ion* 442ff.].) As a result, emphasis falls on Amphitryon's final, brief and biting words against Zeus. Elsewhere in Euripides we find such "challenging prayers" to gods, but this one has special point because of its position in the drama.

[3]The chorus, already in the orchestra, now dances and sings its second song, commonly called the first *stasimon*, "standing song". The song, intended as a *threnos*, a lamentation of the presumed dead Heracles, is more or an *encomium*, a eulogy in praise of his accomplishments, particularly his "labors". Heracles' labors were many, and which of them constituted the canonical twelve varied according to author, time and place. In this song, as frequently, the focus is on Heracles as a benefactor to mankind. The ode has an interesting structure: the repeated metrical pattern of the strophes and antistrophes is the norm, but the repeated short stanzas (called mesode after the strophe and epode after the antistrophe) after each of the stanzas is remarkable. The central ten stanzas of the song each describe one labor, except for Antistrophe b and Mesode c, which describe two each.

[4]Phoebus is another name for the god Apollo, appropriately invoked as a god of song, especially of those played on the lyre.

28

Whether I am to call him the offspring of Zeus
Or of Amphitryon.   355
Excellent deeds achieved with noble toil
Are glory for the dead.

Mesode a
First[1] he rid Zeus' grove
Of the lion,   360
And putting the skin on his back
He covered his blond head
With the dread beast's tawny gaping jaws.

Antistrophe a
And he once laid low with his murderous arrows
The mountain-dwelling race   365
Of savage Centaurs,
Killing them with his winged shafts.[2]
The beautiful-swirling Peneius
And its vast, barren fields
Bear witness to this,
As do the dwellings on Mount Pelion   370
And the neighboring settlements of Mount Homole,
Where filling their hands with pine trees[3]
The Centaurs would subdue the land of Thessalians
By their ridings.

Epode a
And killing the golden-horned,   375
Dappled-back hind,
The scourge of farmers,
He honors the beast-slaying
Goddess of Oenoe.[4]

Strophe b
And he mounted the four-horse chariot   380
And with curbs subdued

---

[1]Subduing the Nemean lion was the canonical first labor. After strangling it to death (its skin was invulnerable), Heracles put on its skin and jaws, and this became his characteristic garb in literature and art. Nemea is in the northern Peloponnese (see map).

[2]On the Centaurs in general, see above, n. on 181. A different group of Centaurs is referred to here, as the geography of this passage (the river Peneius, Mount Homole, etc.) places them in Thessaly and environs (see map).

[3]To use as weapons.

[4]The goddess of Oenoe, located at the border of the Argolid and Arcadia (see map), is Artemis, the goddess of the hunt, to whom the offering of the so-called Cerynitian hind is appropriate.

Diomedes' mares, who in their murderous stalls
Would despatch with unbridled zeal
Bloody meals with their jaws,
Harsh eaters, delighting   385
In human flesh. And he went
Beyond the silver-rich banks
Of the Hebrus,
As he toiled for the lord of Mycenae.[1]

Mesode b
And on the Pelian headland
Along the streams of Anaurus   390
He killed with his arrows
Cycnus,[2] murderer of strangers, Amphanae's
Unsociable inhabitant.

Antistrophe b
And he went to the maidens of song[3]
And their dwelling in the west   395
To pluck by hand the golden fruit
From the apple-bearing leaves,
After killing the tawny-backed serpent,
Who guarded them coiling around
With its coils, unapproachable.
And he travelled into the recesses of the salty   400
Sea, making calm waters
For mortal oarsmen.[4]

Epode b
And going to the home of Atlas[5]
He drove his hands
Under the middle of heaven's vault   405
And held up the starry dwellings

---

[1]The mares of Diomedes were located up north in Thrace (see map), where the Hebrus flowed; Heracles had to subdue these man-eating horses for Eurystheus, the lord of Mycenae.

[2]According to some traditions, Cycnus, a son of the war-god Ares, beheaded strangers on their way to Apollo's shrine at Delphi, and Apollo urged upon Heracles the task of killing him. The geographical references in this passage, however, seem to place the event near Mount Pelion and Amphanae, in Magnesia (see map).

[3]The maidens of song were the Hesperides, dwellers of the far west, whose golden apples were protected by a fierce snake.

[4]The seventh labor in this song is rather unspecifically expressed: Heracles calmed the waters for mortals. Note that this stanza contains two labors.

[5]For Atlas see above, n. on 235. Elsewhere Atlas plucked the golden apples while Heracles held up the world. The chorus gives Heracles credit for both deeds.

Of the gods by his manly strength.

Strophe c

And he went through the hostile swell of sea[1]
To the horse-riding host of Amazons
Around Moetis with its many rivers,   410
Gathering all of his friends
Together from Greece
To pluck the ruinous quarry
Of the gold-decked warrior's belt
From the warlike maiden's robe.   415
And Greece seized the foreign maiden's
Famous spoil, and
It is preserved in Mycenae.

Mesode c

And he burned up the thousand-headed,
Much-destructive hound of Lerna,   420
The hydra,[2]
And smeared its venom on his shafts,
With which he killed the three-bodied
Herdsman of Erytheia.[3]

Antistrophe c

And he both went through other races   425
With glorious success and sailed into
Much-lamented Hades, his final labor,[4]
Where, wretched one, he is finishing off
His life, and he has not come back.
His halls are bereft of friends,   430
And Charon's boat awaits
The children's life's journey,

---

[1] This refers to the Black Sea (the marsh, Moetis, was located north of it), where Heracles did battle with the Amazons, a group of legendary woman warriors, whose leader is alternately called Antiope and Hippolyte. In this battle Heracles was victorious and made off with the leader's belt, often translated as "girdle", which he dedicated at Hera's shrine in Mycenae.

[2] Usually the second labor, the subduing of the Lernean hydra provided Heracles with the venom for his arrows; Lerna was located south of Argos (see map).

[3] The herdsman of Erytheia, located in southwest Spain, was Geryon, a three-bodied or three-headed creature, whose cattle Heracles had to bring to Eurystheus. Note that this Mesode, like Antistrophe b, contains two labors.

[4] Going down into Hades to fetch its watchdog, the multi-headed Cerberus, was Heracles' last labor, the one from which his family and the chorus despair of his returning. Charon (432) was the ferryman of Hades, on whose boat one crossed the river Styx and entered the underworld.

Which has no return, and is god-forsaken
And unjust. The house looks to your[1] arms
And you're not here.   435
Epode c
But if I had the strength of my youth
And could wield the spear in battle,
And were joined by my comrades,
I would champion the children
With might. But as things stand, I lack   440
My blessed youth.

And now I see these people,[2] wearing
The garments of the dead,
The children of the formerly, once great
Heracles, and his loving wife,   445
Pulling beside her their children,
Who cling to her feet which guide them, and the old father of
   Heracles.
I am wretched!
I am no longer able to hold back
My old eyes' tears.   450

*(Megara, with the children clinging to her feet, and Amphitryon have come
forth from the palace.)*

Megara
Well then. Who is the priest, who is the sacrificer of the ill-
   starred?
[Or the murderer of my wretched life?]
These sacrificial victims are ready to be led off to Hades.
Children, we are being led off, a not pretty yoke of corpses,
The old man and the young and their mother all together.   455
Wretched fate, mine and the children's,
These, whom my eyes gaze on for the very last time.
I gave you birth, and I reared you for your enemies
To abuse, laugh at, and destroy.
Oh!
Much have I fallen from my hopeful expectation,   460
Which I once had from your father's words.

---

[1]The chorus is addressing Heracles, even though he's absent; such addresses
are not uncommon in choral songs.

[2]The song has ended and the chorus now announces in anapests the entrance
of the family in their funereal garb. Entrances immediately after choral
songs are generally not announced in Greek tragedy, but are commonly
announced in situations such as this one, the slow and solemn entrance of
a group, a "moving tableau".

To *you*[1] your now dead father used to assign Argos
And you were going to live and rule in Eurystheus' house,
Wielding power over the fertile Pelasgian[2] land;
And he used to put around your head the lion's   465
Skin, with which he used to arm himself.
And *you* were lord of chariot-loving Thebes,
Taking possession of my land as inheritance,
Since you would win over the one who begot you,
And he would place in your right hand his club   470
As protection, finely wrought, a make-believe gift.[3]
And to *you* he promised to give Oechalia,[4]
Which he had once sacked with his well-aimed arrows.
Your father would exalt you three
With three kingdoms, proud in his manly strength.   475
And I would pick out brides
From the land of the Athenians, from Sparta, and
Thebes, contracting marriages, so that moored
By stern cables,[5] you would have a happy life.
But this is all gone: fortune changed   480
And gave you instead Keres[6] to have as brides
And wretched me tears to bear as the ritual bath water.[7]
Your father's father here gives the marriage feast,
Deeming Hades your father-in-law, a bitter marriage tie.
Oh! which of you first, which one last   485
Am I to place aginst my breast? Whose mouth to kiss?
Whom to hold? Would that I like a shrill-winged
Bee could gather the laments from all,
Gather them, and give forth a single flood of tears.
Dearest, if any voice of mortals is heard   490
In Hades, I say this to you, Heracles:
Your father and children are dying, and I am being destroyed,

---

[1]Megara now addresses her three sons in turn.

[2] The adjective Pelasgian here refers to Argos (for which see above, n. on 2).

[3]The club was the symbol of Thebes and hence is appropriately given to the son who was to rule over Thebes; similarly the first son was given Heracles' lion skin since the lion was the symbol of Argos, the land he was to rule over.

[4]There were several different cities called Oechalia; presumably Euripides means the one in Euboea (see map). Heracles had sacked this city because of his passion for the king's daughter, Iole.

[5]Metaphors from sailing are common in Greek literature (and in this play), as one might expect from a seafaring people.

[6]The Keres were dreadful spirits of death.

[7]Ritual baths were customary for both bride and groom prior to the Athenian wedding ceremony.

Who before now was called happy by mortals because of you.
Help! Come! Appear to me even as a shadow!
For coming even as a dream you would be enough,   495
For they are cowards who are killing your children.

Amphitryon
You, keep trying to conciliate those below, woman,[1]
While I throw my hands to heaven and call on you,
Zeus, if you are going to help these children at all,
To save them, since soon you won't be able.   500
And yet you've been called often; I labor in vain,
For death, it seems, is inevitable.
But, old men, life is short;
See that you go through it as pleasurably as you can,
Without pain from morning to night,   505
Since time doesn't know how to preserve
Hopes, but is gone in flight, eagerly tending its own affairs.
Look at me, I who was admired by mortals,
As I accomplished illustrious deeds—but fortune robbed me
In one day, like a wing to the sky. [2]   510
Great prosperity and reputation—I don't know for whom
These are secure. Farewell. Now, comrades,
For the last time you look upon this dear man.

Megara
Ah!
Old man, I see my dearest one—or what am I to say?

Amphitryon
I don't know, daughter; I can't speak.   515

Megara
This is the man we kept hearing was beneath the earth,
Unless I'm seeing a dream in the daylight.
What am I saying? What sort of dream do I see, out of my mind?
This one is no other than your son, old man.
Come on, children, cling to your father's robes,   520
Go, be quick, don't let go, since for you
He is not at all inferior to Zeus Soter.[3]

---

[1]Amphitryon refers to Megara's concluding prayer for Heracles' return from
the underworld.

[2]The phrase seems proverbial for the precariousness of prosperity.

[3]Megara's command, as the ensuing words make clear, is not followed at
once. The conventions of the Athenian stage allowed the action on one part
of the stage to become "fixed" or artificially slow while the action on the
other side took place. Note that Heracles does not address his family until
after giving a customary greeting to the house and after making a brief aside
explaining that he will approach and speak to them.

(Heracles has entered from one of the parodoi.)

Heracles
Greetings, roof and gate of my hearth,
How joyfully I behold you on my return to the light!
Ah! What is this? I see my children before the house   525
With their heads wreathed with the dead's ornaments,
And my wife among a throng of men,
And my father crying at what misfortunes?
Let me draw near and learn from them:
Wife, what strange thing has come to the house?   530

Megara
Dearest of men...

Amphitryon
            You who come as a saving light to your father...

Megara
Have you arrived, were you saved, coming in the nick of time
    for your dear ones?

Heracles
What are you saying? What disturbance do I arrive at, father?

Megara
We were on the verge of being killed. But you, old man, forgive
    me,
If I snatched before you what you ought to be telling this
    man.   535
For the female is somehow more pitiable than males,
And my children were on the verge of death, and I on the verge
    of destruction.

Heracles
Apollo, with what an opening do you begin your speech!

Megara
They're dead—my brothers and aged father.

Heracles
What are you saying? What did he do or what sort of death did
    he meet?   540

Megara
Lycus, the new ruler of the land, killed him.

Heracles
In combat or because the city was sick?

Megara
Because of faction. And he controls Cadmus' mighty seven-
gated city.

Heracles
But how could fear have reached you and the old man?

Megara
He was going to kill your father, me, and the children.   545

Heracles
What are you saying? Why did he fear my orphaned children?

Megara
Lest they some day exact vengeance for Creon's death.

Heracles
What is this adornment of the children, fitting for the dead?

Megara
We are dressed already in these clothes of death.

Heracles
By force you were about to die? I am wretched!   550

Megara
Yes, bereft of friends, and we kept hearing that you were dead.

Heracles
And how did this loss of heart come to you?

Megara
Eurystheus' heralds kept announcing it.

Heracles
But why had you left my house and hearth?

Megara
By force. While your father was ousted from his bed.   555

Heracles
Didn't reverence keep them from dishonoring the old man?

Megara
Reverence? That goddess dwells far from this land.

Heracles
Was I so lacking in friends in my absence?

Megara
What friends does one have in misfortune?

Heracles
Did they despise the battles I endured against the Minyans?   560

Megara
Friendless, I tell you again, is misfortune.

Heracles
> Throw off these hellish wreaths
> And show rescue's gleam in your eyes,
> A dear exchange for the shadow below.
> And I—for now is the time for the work of my hand—   565
> First will go and raze the house
> Of the new ruler, cut off his impious head
> And hurl it for dogs to tear. And whoever of the Cadmeans
> I discover to be bad after benefiting from me,
> With this victorious club I will subdue them,   570
> While others I will tear apart with winged arrows
> And fill the entire Ismenus[1] with the carnage of corpses.
> And the clear flowing of Dirce will be red with blood.
> For whom should I defend more than my wife,
> Children and old father? Farewell labors!   575
> In vain I worked on them rather than these tasks.
> Indeed I ought to risk dying in defense of these children,
> Since they were doing so for their father. Or how can I call it
>   good
> That I did battle with the hydra and lion
> On Eurystheus' missions, but will not toil over my children's 580
> Threatened death?[2] I shall not then
> Be called Heracles the victorious as before.

Chorus Leader
> It is just for a father to help his children
> And aged father and his partner in marriage.

Amphitryon
> It is your nature, my son, to be a friend to your friends   585
> And hate your enemies. But don't be overly eager.

Heracles
> Which of these things is hastier than it should be, father?

Amphitryon
> The ruler has many poor men as allies,
> Who seem prosperous in their own estimation;
> They staged an uprising and destroyed the city   590
> To rob from their neighbors, since their own patrimony
> Was spent and gone and had escaped through their laziness.
> And you were seen approaching the city, and since you were
>   seen, be careful

---

[1]Ismenus was a river and Dirce a stream in Thebes.

[2]Heracles seems to say that he will toil to avert his children's death, threatened by Lycus, but the language also suggests (ironically, not in Heracles' unconscious) that he is laboring to complete their murder.

Lest you have caused the enemy to gather and you fall unexpectedly.

Heracles
I don't care if the whole city saw me.   595
But seeing a bird on an inauspicious perch[1]
I recognized that some pain had fallen against the house,
And so by forethought I entered the land secretly.

Amphitryon
Good. Go inside now, address Hestia[2]
And let your paternal house see your face.   600
The ruler will come in person to drag off and kill
Your wife and children and slaughter me too.
Waiting here you'll have everything
And you'll profit in safety. Don't throw your city into disorder
Before you set this right, child.   605

Heracles
I'll do this, since you've given good advice, I'll go inside the house.
Coming back after some time from the sunless chambers
Of Hades and Kore[3] below, I'll not disdain
To address first the gods in the house.

Amphitryon
Did you really go into Hades' house, child?   610

Heracles
Yes, I led the three-headed beast to the light.

Amphitryon
Conquering it in battle or by the gifts of the goddess?[4]

Heracles
In battle, but I was successful after seeing the rituals of the mysteries.[5]

Amphitryon
And is the beast really in Eurystheus' house?

---

[1]Augury was practiced in the Greek world.
[2]The goddess of the hearth.
[3]Kore, also known as Persephone, was the daughter of the goddess Demeter and Zeus and the bride of Hades.
[4]One version of the story related that Persephone helped Heracles in defeating Cerberus.
[5]The language of this line strongly calls to mind the Eleusinian mysteries, celebrated in Eleusis, a city near Athens, rites which promised a type of "rebirth". Some accounts had it that Heracles was initiated into these mysteries before his trip to the underworld.

Heracles
The grove of the Chthonian[1] and the city of Hermione have
    it.   615

Amphitryon
And Eurystheus doesn't know that you've come up from the
    earth?

Heracles
He doesn't know, since I came to learn the situation here first.

Amphitryon
Why were you under the earth for so long?

Heracles
I spent time bringing back Theseus from Hades, father.[2]

Amphitryon
And where is he? Has he gone to his fatherland?   620

Heracles
He's gone to Athens, glad to have escaped from below.
But come on, children, accompany your father into the house.
So your entrances into it are fairer
Than your exits from it, right? But be brave,
And shed no more tears.   625
And you, my wife, compose yourself,
Stop trembling, and, all of you, let go of my robes.
I'm not winged and I don't intend to flee my dear ones.
Ah!
The children don't let go, but cling to my robes
So much more. Did you come so close to the razor's edge? 630
Taking them by the hand I will lead these little boats
And like a ship I will pull them in tow; for I do not refuse
The care of my children. All mortals are equal:
They love their children, both the well-born
And those of no account. They differ in money: 635
Some have it, others don't; but everyone loves his children.

(Heracles exits with the children into the palace; Amphitryon and Megara follow them in.)

---

[1]"The Chthonian" is Demeter, the fertility goddess in whose honor the Eleusinian mysteries were held; she also had a shrine at Hermione, near Troezen (see map).

[2]Theseus, the ruler of Athens, had gotten stuck in Hades when he tried to help his friend Pirithous abduct Persephone, and he was rescued by Heracles.

39

Chorus:[1]
Strophe a
  Youth is dear to me;
  But old age, a constant burden
  Heavier than the crags of Aetna,[2]
  Lies on the head, covering over   640
  And darkening my eyes' light.
  May I have neither the wealth
  Of an Asian[3] empire
  Nor my house full of gold,   645
  Have them instead of youth,
  Which is fairest in wealth,
  Fairest in poverty.
  Painful and murderous old age
  I hate. May it perish into   650
  The waves! Would that it had never
  Come to the homes and cities
  Of mortals, but always let it be borne off
  Through the sky on wings.
Antistrophe a
  If the gods had intelligence   655
  And wisdom regarding men's affairs,
  Those who excel would win a double youth,[4]
  A clear sign of their excellence,
  And after their death   660
  They would run a double course and
  Come back to the rays of the sun;
  But the ignoble would have
  A single life to live.
  And by this it would be possible to recognize
  Both the bad and the good,   665
  Just as among the clouds
  Sailors can count the stars.
  But as things are now, there is no marker from the gods
  That is clear for the noble and the base.   670
  But a lifetime as it rolls along

---

[1]The previous song was a type of lament (a *threnos*); this one is a type of epinician, a victory song for Heracles who has triumphantly returned from the underworld.

[2]Aetna is a volcanic moutain on the island of Sicily; the monster Typhoeus was thought to dwell under it.

[3]Asia was proverbial for its wealth.

[4]This notion, perhaps strange-seeming to us, is found elsewhere in Euripides (*Supplices* 1080ff.).

Only increases wealth.
Strophe b
I will not cease mixing together
The Graces and the Muses,[1]
The sweetest yoking. 675
May I never live without music,[2]
But may I always be crowned.[3]
An old singer, I still
Celebrate Mnemosyne,
I still sing 680
Heracles' victory song
Beside the wine-giving Bromius,[4]
Beside the song of the seven-toned lyre
And the Libyan[5] pipe.
In no way will I abandon 685
The Muses, who set me dancing.
Antistrophe b
The Delian maidens[6] around the temples' doors
Whirling in their beautiful dances
Sing a paean[7] in praise
Of Leto's noble child. 690
I will sing paeans in celebration
At your[8] house,
An old singer, like a swan
From a white throat.[9] For what is good
Provides themes for hymns. 695

---

[1]The Muses were the patrons of poets and the source of poetic inspiration. Their mother was Mnemosyne (see 679 below), the personification of memory. The Graces were personifications of loveliness and grace.

[2]The word translated "without music", *amousias*, suggests both without music and without the Muses.

[3]The crowning is both a sign of devotion and a reference to the crown of the victor.

[4]Bromius, "the roarer", is a cult name for Dionysus, the god of wine and ecstatic experience.

[5]The wood of the Libyan lotus tree was said to be good for making the pipe (*aulos*).

[6]Delos, a tiny island in the Aegean sea, was the birthplace of Apollo and an important site for his worship.

[7]The paean was a song particularly associated with Apollo, "Leto's noble child".

[8]"Your" refers to Heracles; see above, n. on 434.

[9]The swan was sacred to Apollo at Delos and was also associated with singers (see above n. on 111). The "white throat" refers to the chorus of old men as well as to the swan.

He is the child of Zeus. Surpassing
In excellence more than in noble birth,
With toil he made life
Calm for mortals
By destroying terrifying beasts.   700

*(Lycus arrives with attendants from the parodos he previously used, just as
or just after Amphitryon enters from the palace.)*[1]

Lycus
Just in time, Amphitryon, you come out of the house;
For a long time now you've been adorning yourselves
With garments and ornaments of the dead.
But come now and tell Heracles' children and wife
To appear outside this house;   705
On these conditions you promised to die voluntarily.

Amphitryon
Lord, you persecute me when I'm in a wretched state
And you mistreat me outrageously now that he's dead;
You ought, even if you hold sway, to strive for this moderately.
But since you are compelling us to die,   710
We must acquiesce; may what you wish be done.

Lycus
Where then is Megara? Where are the children of Alcmene's
    child?

Amphitryon
I think that she, to judge from outside...

Lycus
What's this? What opinion do you hold with certainty?

Amphitryon
She's sitting as a suppliant at the holy altar of Hestia[2]...   715

Lycus
To no purpose she supplicates to save her life.

Amphitryon
And she is calling on her dead husband in vain.

Lycus
He's not here and will *never* come.

---

[1]The following scene is very short, as the action culminating in Lycus' murder
moves rapidly. It involves one of Euripides' favorite patterns, the deception
of someone who is led into the *skene*, where another or others wait in
ambush.
[2]For Hestia see above, n. on 599.

Amphitryon

No, unless one of the gods should raise him up.

Lycus

Go to her and bring her out of the house.   720

Amphitryon

If I did that, I'd be a partner in the murder.

Lycus

Well, since you have this scruple,
I, who lack these fears, will bring forth
The children along with their mother. Come, follow, attendants,
So that we can gladly see a respite from these toils.   725

(Lycus and attendants exit into the palace.)

Amphitryon

You, then, go, go where you should. The rest perhaps
Another will take care of. Expect, if you act badly,
To fare badly.[1] Old men, opportunely
He goes and he will be trapped by sword-bearing
Men and nets, thinking that he'll kill those near him,   730
The utterly evil man. And I'm off so I may see the corpse
Fall. For an enemy's death as he pays the penalty
For his deeds affords pleasure.

(Amphitryon exits into the palace)

Chorus:[2]

—A change from ills! The former lord gloriously   735
Turns his life back from Hades.
Oh,
Justice and the lot from the gods which flows back again!

—Finally you went where you will pay in death the penalty   740
For treating your betters with outrage.

—Joy makes me shed tears.

---

[1] After these words Amphitryon, whose language in this scene up to this point has been misleading, explicitly predicts the murder which awaits Lycus. Lycus and his attendants have probably already entered the *skene* at this point, but even if they have not, the conventions of the Greek theater permitted such "words at the back" which the audience would hear, while the departing character(s) would not.

[2] At this point begins a brief "epirrhematic" scene, in which the chorus in song alternates with an actor in spoken rhythms (Lycus from within); the third *stasimon* proper commences at 763. The choral parts in this section (734-62) are probably sung by individual members of the chorus.

He came back,
Which never before in my thoughts would I have expected   745
To experience, the lord of the land.

—But, old men, let us examine also the events within
The house—to see if someone fares as I wish.

Lycus *(within)*
Oh! Woe is me!

Chorus
—This song begins in the house, dear   750
For me to hear. Death is not far off.
The ruler cries out,
Groaning the prelude of murder.

Lycus *(within)*
Entire land of Cadmus, I am being killed by stealth.

Chorus
—Yes, for you were trying to kill; endure paying fully   755
The retribution, paying the penalty for your deeds.

—What mortal, staining the gods with lawlessness,
Spread the mindless tale
About the blessed Olympians,[1] that the gods
Do not hold power.

—Old men, the impious man is no more.   760
The house is quiet. Let us turn to dances.
[The friends whom I wish are successful.]

Chorus:[2]
Strophe a
Dances, dances
And festivals are celebrated
Throughout the holy city of Thebes.
Changes from tears,   765
Changes of fortune
Give birth to songs.
The new king is gone, and the former one
Holds sway, leaving the harbor of Acheron.[3]   770
Hope came beyond expectations.

---

[1]The Olympians are the gods who dwell on Mount Olympus, the generation of Zeus; they are the chief Greek gods.

[2]The third *stasimon*. The chorus is convinced of divine justice and of Zeus' paternity of Heracles because he has returned successfuly and killed the villian Lycus.

[3]Acheron was one of the rivers of the underworld.

44

Antistrophe a
The gods, the gods
Take care to heed
The unjust and the holy.
Gold and good fortune,
Bringing with them unjust power,   775
Lead mortals from their senses.
For no one dares to look to the future
As he neglects the law and favors lawlessness.
He smashes the dark chariot of wealth.   780

Strophe b
Ismenus,[1] be garlanded,
And polished streets of the seven-gated
City and beautiful-flowing Dirce,
Start the dancing,
And, leaving your father's water,   785
Nymphs, daughters of Asopus,[2] join me in singing
The victorious contest
Of Heracles.
Wooded rock of the Pythian,[3]   790
And home of the Heliconian[4] Muses,
Extol with joyous sound
My city, my walls,
Where the race of Spartoi[5] appeared,
A band of bronze-shielded warriors, who handed down 795
The land to their children's children;
They are a holy light for Thebes.

Antistrophe b
Two kindred marriage
Beds, mortal and
Of Zeus, who came to the bed   800
Of Perseus' granddaughter.[6] How
Believable to me was your long-ago union

---

[1]For Ismenus and Dirce, see above, n. on 572.

[2]The daughters of Asopus are the river divinities, nymphs, descended from the river god Asopus; the river ran near Thebes.

[3]This refers to Mount Parnassus (see above n. on 240), the home of Pythian Apollo and the Muses.

[4] Mount Helicon in Boeotia (see map) was another home of the Muses.

[5]For the Spartoi, see above n. on 5.

[6]Perseus' granddaughter was Alcmene. Note that the vocative which begins this stanza is never picked up; such "hanging vocatives" are not uncommon in choral poetry.

Revealed, Zeus, when it seemed unlikely.
Time revealed brightly   805
The might of Heracles,
Who came forth from the chambers of the earth,
Leaving the nether home of Pluto.[1]
You[2] were a better ruler to me
Than the ignoble lord,   810
Who now, looking on the contest
Of swords, makes clear
Whether justice
Still pleases the gods.[3]

(The figures of Iris and Lyssa appear on high.)[4]

—Ah! Ah!   815
Do we have the same fear,
Old men, since I see such a phantom above the house?

—In flight, in flight
Raise your sluggish limbs, get out of the way.

—Lord Paean[5]   820
May you avert pains from us.

Iris
Don't be afraid, old men, in seeing this offspring of Night,
Lyssa, and me, the servant of the gods,
Iris; for we come with no harm to the city,
But against one man's house we wage war,   825
Who they say is from Zeus and Alcmene.
Until he fully completed his bitter trials
Necessity was keeping him safe, nor would his father Zeus
Allow either me or Hera to harm him at any time.

---

[1]Pluto is another name for Hades.
[2]The chorus addresses Heracles; see above, n. on 434.
[3]The song which confidently asserts belief in the justice of the gods, a theodicy, concludes with "proof" of this—Heracles' victory over Lycus. The concluding "Whether justice still pleases the gods" is rhetorical on the part of the chorus, but the following appearance of Iris and Lyssa "answers" this rhetorical proposition.
[4]Iris, the messenger god, and Lyssa, whose name means "madness", which she personifies, appear on high, most probably in the *mechane* (see *Introduction*, 6), which causes the fearful cries of the chorus. (The chariot referred to by the chorus at 880 is most likely not physically present, only metaphorically.) This appearance of the gods in mid-play is most surprising (see *Interpretation*, 77). And nowhere else is there a more violent rupture between a song and the following action.
[5]Paean is a name for Apollo in his capacity as a healing god.

But since he's gone through the toils of Eurystheus,   830
Hera wishes to attach to him kindred blood
By his killing of the children, and I wish the same.
But come then, pull together your implacable heart,
Unmarried maiden of dark Night,
And against this man drive, stir up   835
Fits of madness, disturbances of mind to kill his children,
And leapings of his feet; let out the murderous cable
So that conveying through Acheron's[1] strait
His crown of beautiful children, killed in familial murder,
He may recognize what sort is Hera's anger against him   840
And learn mine. Otherwise the gods are nowhere
And mortal things will be great, if he doesn't pay the penalty.[2]

Lyssa

I am sprung from a noble father and mother,
From Night and the blood of Uranus.[3]
I hold an office that the gods don't like to admire   845
And I don't delight in going against mortals dear to me.
But before seeing her stumble I wish
To advise Hera and you, in the hope that you heed my words.
This man, whose house you send me against,
Is not undistiguished either on earth or among the gods.   850
Taming the desolate land and savage sea,
He alone restored the honors
Of the gods which fell at the hands of impious men.
And so I advise you not to plot great evils.

Iris: [4]

Don't you give advice about Hera's and my plans.   855

Lyssa

I'm trying to lead your step to the better instead of evil.

Iris

Zeus' wife didn't send you here to be sensible.

---

[1]On Acheron, see above, n. on 770.

[2]This line has often been interpreted to mean that Heracles is to be punished for "hubris", arrogant behavior, towards the gods. Neither this line nor the play supports this view. (See *Intrepretation*, 77-78.)

[3]Uranus was the sky god two generations before Zeus.

[4]At this point the meter shifts to trochaic tetrameters, a rhythm often used to express excitement.

Lyssa

I call on Helius[1] to witness that I'm doing what I don't wish to
do.
But if indeed it's necessary for me to serve Hera and you,
Yes, I'll go. Neither is the sea so fierce as it moans with
   waves   860
Nor an earthquake nor the raging thunderbolt breathing forth
   pangs
As the race I'll run against Heracles' chest;
And I'll smash his halls and hurl the house on him,
After I've killed the children first. And the killer[2] will not
   know   865
That he's slain the children he begot until he casts off my mad-
   ness.
There, look. See, he's tossing his head from the starting line[3]
And in silence he twists and distorts his Gorgon-gleaming eyes
And cannot control his breathing, and like a bull set to charge,
He roars horribly. I call up the Keres of Tartarus[4]   870
To screech at once and accompany me like dogs a huntsman.
Soon I will set you[5] dancing all the more and play for you a pipe
   of fear.
Iris, raise your noble foot and go to Olympus,
While I enter the house of Heracles unseen.

(Lyssa and Iris exit separately.)[6]

Chorus:[7]

Otototoi , groan! The bloom of your city,   875
The child of Zeus is cut off,
Wretched Greece, you who will lose,

---

[1]Helius, the sun god, was frequently called to witness because he could
literally oversee everything.

[2]Lyssa claims that both she and Heracles will be the murderers of the children.
On such "double determination" see below, n. on 1135.

[3]Heracles is imagined in the initial stages of madness, first as a runner in a
race, then a bull.

[4]Tartarus is the underworld; for the Keres, see above, n. on 481.

[5]"You" is addressed to Heracles.

[6]Lyssa dismounts from the *mechane* to the roof of the *skene* and probably
descends via a ladder at the back of the stage building; Iris exits on the
machine.

[7]The following lines (875-921) fall into three sections: the chorus alone
(875-85), the chorus with Amphitryon speaking from within (886-909), and
the chorus with the "messenger"(910-21). The predominant rhythm is
dochmiac, which typically indicates, as it does here, great excitement.

Will lose your benefactor, set to dancing
By a raging madness singing in his ears.

The most grievous one is gone in her chariot   880
And lays the goad
On the horses to cause ruin,
A Gorgon[1] of Night with the hissing of
A hundred snakes, Lyssa with the petrifying gaze.

In a moment a divinity overturns the fortunate,
In a moment the children will breathe their last at their father's
    hands.   885

Amphitryon *(within)*
Oh, wretched me!

Chorus
Oh Zeus, the Poinai,[2] crazed, eating raw flesh,
Acting unjustly, will at once lay low your race
With ills and make it childless.

Amphitryon *(within)*
Oh roof!

Chorus
The dances without drums begin,
Not pleasing to the thyrsus of Bromius.[3]   890

Amphitryon *(within)*
Oh house!

Chorus
The spirits go for blood, not for the streams
Of a Dionysian libation of wine.

Amphitryon *(within)*
In flight, children, away!

Chorus
                This is a ruinous song,
Ruinous, which is played upon the pipe.   895
He hunts down and pursues his children. Never will Lyssa revel
Without accomplishment in the house.

Amphitryon: *(within)*
Aiai, the ills!

---

[1]For Gorgon see above, n. on 131; here it is used figuratively.

[2]The Poinai are personifications of vengeance.

[3]The thyrsus was a staff entwined with ivy or grape vines and tipped with a
   pine cone. It was used in the worship of Dionysus, who was known also by
   the title Bromius, "the roaring one". Note here and elsewhere the Dionysiac
   and music images in connection with Heracles' madness.

Chorus
Yes, *aiai*! How I grieve for the old 900
Father, and the mother, whose
Children were born in vain.
Look, look, a storm shakes the house, the roof collapses.[1] 905

Amphitryon (*within*)
Look, look! What are you doing in the house, child of Zeus?
You send a hellish disturbance against the house, Pallas,
As once you did against Enceladus.[2]

(Enter messenger from the palace.)[3]

Messenger
You who are white with age...

Chorus
                              What shout do you 910
Call me with?

Messenger
                    Insufferable things for the house.

Chorus
                                        I will send for
No second prophet.

Messenger
The children are dead.

Chorus
                    Aiai!

---

[1] The collapse of the palace probably was not indicated by any special effects but left to the audience to imagine. It is assumed within the play to have occurred.

[2] Pallas Athena once subdued the Giant Enceladus. Her appearance here is beneficent as she prevents Heracles from parricide. Just as the audience is asked to imagine the collapse of the palace, so too they are asked to imagine the sudden appearance of the goddess Athena described by Amphitryon; she was not visible on stage.

[3] The "messenger" emerges from the palace and provides to the chorus and audience news of what happened within. So far all the audience knows is Lyssa's plans, cries from within and the intervention of Athena. The following scene with its long narrative provides the details of Heracles' murder of his family. "Messenger" is a traditional, although somewhat misleading, name for the character who offers news, not messages; here he is a household servant. Since violent actions and other, difficult-to-stage events, were only rarely enacted on the tragic stage, this character was very useful for providing such information.

Messenger
Lament what is truly lamentable.

Chorus
                 Ruinous murders,
Ruinous hands of a parent.   915

Messenger
One could not say more than we have suffered.

Chorus
How did the father's lamentable madness, mad destruction,
Which you reveal, come upon the children?
Explain in what way these ills from a god
Rushed against the house,   920
And make clear the wretched fortunes of the children.

Messenger:[1]
There were rituals before the hearth of Zeus,[2]
Purifications for the house, since Heracles had killed
The land's ruler and thrown him out of this house.
And the beautiful band of children was standing around
    him,   925
And so were his father and Megara, and already the basket had
    circled
Around the altar, and we were keeping a holy silence.
As he was about to take the burning torch with his right hand
To dip it into the water, Alcmene's child
Stood in silence. And as their father delayed   930
The children looked at him; and he was no longer himself,
But diseased in the rolling of his eyes
And after sprouting bloodshot veins in his eyes
He was dripping down froth from his thick beard
And he spoke with deranged laughter,   935
"Father, why do I sacrifice with purifying fire
Before killing Eurystheus, and have twice the trouble?
To set these things right is the work of a single blow of my hand.
And when I bring here Eurystheus' head
I'll purify my hands of the present murder.   940
Pour out the libations, throw the baskets from your hands.
Who'll give me my bow and arrows? Who my hand's weapon?
I'll go to Mycenae; I must seize
Crowbars and axes to totally shatter with iron tools

---

[1] The rhythm returns to iambic trimeter.
[2] Heracles begins the rituals of purification (involving the basket, containing barley and a knife, and a torch) needed to cleanse himself of Lycus' blood. The need for purification does not imply moral guilt.

The Cyclopean foundations,[1] fitted together   945
With lines marked in red and with chisels."
After this, walking he claimed that he had a chariot,
Not having one, and he was mounting the chariot's rail,
And he was striking with his hand as if, I suppose, with a goad.
The servants felt both fear and laughter together,   950
And looking at one another they said,
"Is our master teasing us or is he mad?"
But he was going back and forth throughout the house,
And rushing into the middle of the men's quarters,[2] he claimed
He had arrived at the city of Nisus[3] , and standing inside the
    house   955
And lying down on the ground, just as he was, he prepared him-
    self
A meal. After delaying for a short time
He said he was going to the wooded plains of the Isthmus.
And then he stripped off his garments
And was competing against no one, and himself by himself   960
Was being proclaimed victor over no one, after demanding
An audience.[4] Roaring terribly against Eurystheus
He was in Mycenae by his account. His father,
Taking him by his mighty hand, addressed him:
"Child, what's wrong? What is the nature of this aberration? 965
Surely it's not that the bloodshed of those
You just killed has made you frenzied?"[5] But he, thinking it was
    Eurystheus'
Father trembling as a suppliant to touch his hand,
Pushed him away, and prepared his ready quiver
And arrows for his own children, thinking he was killing   970
Those of Eurystheus. They, trembling with fear,
Were darting, one here, one there, one to his poor mother's
Robes, another beneath a pillar's shadow,
And another cowered like a bird under the altar.
Their mother cried out, "You begot them, what are you doing?
    Are you killing   975

---

[1]On the Cyclopean foundations, see above, n. on 16.
[2]Men and women had separate quarters in a Greek house of Euripides' time.
[3]The city of Nisus is Megara on the Isthmus of Corinth (see 957 below and the map), so called after its king Nisus.
[4]Corinth, where Heracles imagines he is, was the site of athletic games, the Isthmian games, every two years.
[5]The Greeks believed that bloodshed could cause madness; that is not what caused Heracles' frenzy here.

Your children?" And the old man and the crowd of servants
    called out,
But he, twisting his child in a circle away from the pillar,
A terrible turning by the foot, stood opposite
And struck him in the liver. And on his back, the boy
Breathing out his life, drenched the stone pillars.   980
But his father raised a shout and added this boast:
"This one dead nestling of Eursytheus
Has fallen at my hands, paying fully for his father's hatred."
And he was aiming his bow at another, who had cowered
Around the altar's foundation, thinking that he was hidden. 985
And the wretch fell at his father's knees first,
And throwing his hand towards his father's chin and neck[1]
Said, "Dearest, father, don't kill me;
I am yours, your child, you won't be killing Eurystheus'."
But he, since the child stood within the ruinous bow's range, 990
Rolling his wild-looking Gorgon's eyes,
Raised his club above his head, like a smith forging iron,
Struck it against the child's blond head,
And shattered the bones. After killing the second child,
He went to sacrifice a third victim in addition to these two. 995
But first the wretched mother carried him off
Inside the house and locked the doors.
But he, as if at the Cyclopean walls themselves,
Was digging and levering the door frames, and tearing out the
    posts
Laid low wife and child in one shot.   1000
And then he galloped towards his father's murder.
But a phantom came, as it appeared to view
Pallas, brandishing a spear over her helmet's crest,
And she threw a rock aginst Heracles' chest,
Which checked him from his raging murder and sent him 1005
Into sleep; he fell to the ground, striking his back
Against a pillar, which had broken in two
In the roof's collapse and was lying on the foundations.
But we, freed from our flight,
With the old man's help, attached bonds of twisted knots 1010
To the pillar, so that when he ceased from sleep
He would not do anying in addition to these deeds.
And the wretch sleeps an unblessed sleep,
After killing his children and wife. And for my part, I
Don't know who of mortals is more miserable.   1015

(The messenger exits either back into the palace or down one of the parodoi.)

---

[1]The gestures described are the traditional ones of supplication.

Chorus:[1]
There was a murder which the rock of Argos[2] keeps,
Then most infamous and unbelievable to Greece—
That of Danaus' children;[3]
But these deeds of the wretched son of Zeus
Surpassed, outstripped those former ills.   1020

I am able to tell of Procne's[4] murder of one child,
Sacrificed to the Muses; but you, begetting
Three children, destroyer,
Joined a raging mad lot in killing them.

Aiai! What lamentation   1025
Or wailing or song of the dead or what
Dance of Hades am I to sound?

Ah! Ah!
Look, the doors of the high-gated
House are parting.[5]   1030
Oh me!
Look at the miserable children
Lying before their wretched father,
Who sleeps a terrible sleep after the children's murder,
And around Heracles' body   1035
There are these bonds
And many strong knots, attached
To the stony pillar of the house.

And the old man, like a bird lamenting its pangs
Over its unfledged children, following   1040

---

[1]The chorus now sings a brief, astrophic song in which they compare Heracles' deeds to those of previous mythological characters familiar to the audience. Such use of *exempla* is common in Greek poetry. Here it allows the chorus/Euripides to underscore the horror of the deeds.

[2]The rock of Argos is the citadel of the city of Argos.

[3]With the exception of the eldest, Hypermnestra, all fifty daughters of Danaus, after being forced to marry their cousins, killed them on their wedding night.

[4]Procne, in order to take vengeance on her husband Tereus for his rape and brutal treatment of her sister Philomela, killed their son, Itys. It remains unclear why the son is said to be sacrificed to the Muses.

[5]Although there is still some debate on the issue, it is very likely that here the device known as the *ekkyklema* (see *Introduction*,6-7) was used. It would allow the audience now to see the interior scene described by the messenger: the corpses of the children and Megara and the sleeping and bound Heracles. Amphitryon, who is not part of this tableau, follows the *ekkyklema* on foot and is announced in iambic trimeters by the chorus at 1039-41.

54

With bitter steps, is here.

(Amphitryon enters from the palace, following the ekkyklema with the corpses and the sleeping Heracles.)[1]

Amphitryon
  Old men of Cadmus, in silence, in silence
  Will you not let this man relaxed in sleep
  Forget his ills completely?

Chorus
  Old man, with tears I groan over you, and   1045
  The children and the victor.

Amphitryon
  Move farther off, don't
  Make a sound, don't shout, don't
  Rouse him from his bed
  While he rests calmly   1050
  In sleep.

Chorus
            Oimoi!
  How much bloodshed this is...

Amphitryon
                                    Ah, ah! You'll destroy me.

Chorus
                                              That has
  Been spilled and rises up.

Amphitryon
  Won't you cry out a silent
  Lamentation, old men?
  Or he'll wake up, loosen the bonds, and destroy the city,   1055
  Destroy his father and shatter the house.

Chorus
  It's impossible, impossible for me.

Amphitryon
  Silence, let me listen to his breathing. Come, let me lend an
      ear.   1060

Chorus
  Is he sleeping?

---

[1]The following scene (up to 1086) is a charged lyric scene between the chorus and Amphitryon, of which the central theme is the fear of an awakened Heracles. There is considerable movement in this scene, with Amphitryon trying to get the chorus to be quiet and to move away from the sleeping Heracles and Amphitryon himself moving away in fear (see 1070 and 1081ff.).

Amphitryon
> Yes, he sleeps an accursed sleep that is no sleep,
He who killed his wife, killed his children
With the twang of the bow.

Chorus
Now groan…

Amphitryon
> I groan.

Chorus
The destruction of the children…

Amphitryon
> *Oimoi!*   1065

Chorus
And of your child…

Amphitryon
> *Aiai!*

Chorus
Old man.

Amphitryon
> Silence, silence!
He's awake, he's turning over. Come,
I'll conceal myself, hidden within the house.   1070

(Amphitryon moves away from Heracles.)

Chorus
Courage. Night holds your son's eyelids.

Amphitryon
Look out, look out. Wretched,
In my woes I don't shrink from leaving
The light, but I'm afraid that if he slays me, his father,   1075
He'll contrive ills on top of ills
And have more kindred bloodshed
In addition to these Erinyes.[1]

Chorus
You should have died then, when you came home
After punishing the murder of your wife's brother
By sacking the very famous city of the Taphians.   1080

---

[1] The Erinyes were spirits of punishment, especially of kindred bloodshed. Amphitryon means that Heracles, if he kills his father, will incur more spirits of vengeance, in addition to those he has from the murder of his children.

Amphitryon
  Flight, flight, old men, move away from
  The house. Flee the mad
  Man who's waking.
  Or soon, throwing a second murder on top of murder,   1085
  He'll be frenzied again throughout the city of Cadmeans.

(Amphitryon flees from the waking Heracles.)

Chorus
  Zeus, why did you hate your child
  So cruelly and lead him into this sea of ills?

Heracles:[1]
  Ah!
  I'm alive and I see what I ought to see,
  The sky and the earth and these shafts of the sun.   1090
  But how I've fallen into a billowy and terrible
  Disturbance of my wits and I'm drawing hot breaths,
  Shallow ones, not securely from the lungs.
  Look, why with my vigorous trunk and arms
  Moored like a ship with bonds   1095
  Do I sit against stonework that is broken in two,
  Sitting next to corpses?
  My winged shafts and bow are strewn on the ground,
  Which before now stood beside my arms
  And protected my sides and were protected by me.   1100
  Surely I haven't descended again back into Hades,
  After completing the course from Hades for Eurysthesus?
  But I see neither the Sisyphean rock[2]
  Nor Pluto nor the scepters of Demeter's daughter.
  I'm astounded. Where in the world am I that I'm at a loss? 1105
  Hello! Who of my friends is near or far
  To cure this ignorance of mine?
  For I recognize nothing clearly of what I'm used to.

Amphitryon
  Old men, shall I draw near my woes?

---

[1]Heracles gradually comes to and begins to recognize his surroundings. He remains confused, however, and more information will come from Amphitryon, who slowly reenters the scene, after fleeing his son at 1081ff.

[2]Sisyphus was a notorious sinner, punished in the underworld by being compelled to roll a rock up a hill, only to have it roll down again *ad infinitum*. Heracles, entertaining the possibility that he might have returned to Hades, remarks that he sees none of the familiar sights, Sisyphus' rock, Pluto (see above, n. on 808) or the scepters of Demeter's daughter (see above, n. on 608).

Chorus
And I with you, I won't abandon these misfortunes.   1110
Heracles
Father, why do you weep and cover your eyes,
Standing far away from your dearest child?
Amphitryon
Child, yes, even though you're badly off you are mine.
Heracles
What pain do I suffer, which you're crying over?
Amphitryon
Things that even a god, should he learn of them, would
        lament.   1115
Heracles
The boast is great, but you haven't yet named the misfortune.
Amphitryon
No, for you yourself can see, if you're now sane.
Heracles
Tell me if you're adding some strange new thing to my life.
Amphitryon
If you're no longer a hellish reveller, I'd explain.
Heracles
Ah! Again you've spoken this curious riddle.   1120
Amphitryon
Yes, I'm examining whether you're now firmly sane.
Heracles
I don't recall at all my mind being frenzied.
Amphitryon
Should I loosen my child's bonds, old men, or what am I to do?[1]
Heracles
And tell me who bound me; for I feel ashamed.
Amphitryon
Know this much of your ills; leave the rest alone.   1125
Heracles
Is silence enough for what I wish to learn?
Amphitryon
Zeus, do you see these things from Hera's throne?[2]

---

[1]At this point, it seems, Amphitryon unbinds Heracles.
[2]Amphitryon's remark suggests Zeus' subservience to Hera's wishes in this
   matter.

Heracles

But have we suffered something hostile from that quarter?

Amphitryon

Let the goddess be and take care of your own ills.

Heracles

I'm ruined; you'll speak of some misfortune.   1130

Amphitryon

Look, behold these fallen corpses of children.

Heracles

Oimoi! What is this sight I see in my wretchedness?

Amphitryon

You strove after, my son, a war that was no war against the children.

Heracles

What war did you mean? Who killed them?

Amphitryon

You and your bow and arrows and the god who is
responsible.[1]   1135

Heracles

What are you saying? What did I do? Father, you're announcing ills.

Amphitryon

You were mad. You're asking for painful explanations.

Heracles

Am I the murderer of my wife too?

Amphitryon

All these deeds are of your hand alone.

Heracles

Aiai! A cloud of lamentation surrounds me.   1140

Amphitryon

For these reasons I lament your fortunes.

Heracles

Did I smash my house where I raged in madness?

---

[1]The role of the god does not remove Heracles' own responsibility for these deeds. The Greeks accepted a notion of "double" or "over" determination for actions: a divine agent as well as a mortal share the responsibility. Here are named mortal agent, god, and weapon.

Amphitryon
I know nothing except one thing: everything of yours is in
misfortune.

Heracles
Where did the sting of madness seize me? Where did it destroy
me?

Amphitryon
When you were purifying your hands with fire around
the altar. 1145

Heracles
Oimoi! Why do I spare my life,
Since I've become the murderer of my dearest children?
Shall I not go to leap from a smooth rock
Or by striking a sword into my liver
Become an avenger of my children's blood, 1150
Or by kindling my vigorous flesh with fire
Thrust away my life's infamy which remains.
But interrupting my thoughts of suicide
Here comes Theseus, my kin[1] and friend.
I'll be seen and the pollution[2] of child murder 1155
Will come to the eyes of the dearest of my friends.[3]
Oimoi, what shall I do? Where am I to find solitude from
Ills, taking wing or going beneath the earth?
Come, I'll throw a shadow around my head,
For I'm ashamed at the evils I've done, 1160
And I wish in no way afflict the blameless
By striking this man with blood guilt.

(Heracles covers his head.)

(Theseus has entered from one of the parodoi.)[4]

---

[1]Theseus was Heracles' cousin on both his mother's and father's (Zeus')
sides.

[2]Pollution, it was believed, could be spread by contact and even by sight or
hearing.

[3]The word *xenos*, translated here in the plural as "friends", means stranger,
guest and host. Here it refers to the friendship which develops in the context of
the host-guest relationship, an important one for the Greeks, and one protected
by no less a power than Zeus himself.

[4]Theseus' arrival is a mild surprise; we have heard of his return from Hades
earlier in the play, but there was no reason to expect that he would arrive
at this crucial juncture. He has "partial vision" upon entrance, seeing
initially only part of the stage.

60

Theseus

I arrive with others, who remain along the streams
Of the Asopus,[1] armed soldiers of the land of the Athenians,
Bearing, old man, an allied force to your child.   1165
For a report came to the city of the sons of Erechtheus[2]
That Lycus had snatched this land's scepter
And was waging war and battle against you.
And making a return for what Heracles began
In saving me from below, I have come, old man, if you have 1170
Any need of my hand or of my allies'.
Ah! Why is the ground full of these corpses?
It can't be that I've been left behind and have arrived
Too late for these unexpected ills. Who killed these children?
Whose wife was this I see?   1175
Children don't stand near the spear;
No, I discover, doubtless, some other new ill.

Amphitryon

Lord who holds the olive-bearing hill...[3]

Theseus

Why do you address me with a pitiable[4] prelude?

Amphitryon

We have suffered miserable sufferings at the hands of the
    gods.   1180

Theseus

These children over whom you cry, whose are they?

Amphitryon

My suffering offspring begot them,
And their begetter, enduring bloodshed's pollution, slew them.

Theseus

What are you saying? What did he do?

Amphitryon

                    Deranged by an impulse of madness   1185
With arrows dipped in the hundred-headed hydra's blood.[5]

---

[1]For the Asopus, see above, n. on 786.
[2]Erechtheus was one of the legendary early kings of Athens.
[3]From 1178-1213 the exchange between Amphitryon and Theseus is in lyric, predominantly dochmiac, rhythms, again indicating excitement. "Olive-bearing hill" refers to Athens, famous for its olive industry.
[4]Pitiable, probably because of the music which accompanied the address, not because of the words themselves.
[5] See above, n. on 421.

Theseus
You've spoken dreadful things.

Amphitryon
We're gone, gone, nothing.

Theseus
Speak no ill-omened word.

Amphitryon
You command one wishing so.

Theseus
This contest is Hera's. But who is this among the corpses, old
    man?

Amphitryon
This one is mine, my much-suffering child, who went   1190
To the plain of Phlegra[1] as a warrior with the gods
To the battle where the Giants were killed.

Theseus
Oh! Oh! Who of men is so ill-starred by nature?   1195

Amphitryon
You couldn't know another mortal
Who has suffered more and been forced to wander more.

Theseus
Why does he cover his miserable head with his robes?

Amphitryon
Feeling shame before your eyes
And before your friendship and kinship   1200
And at the murder of his children.

Theseus
But if I came to share the pain? Uncover him.

Amphitryon
My child, drop the robe
From your eyes, throw it off, show your face to the sun.
My weight joins my tears in wrestling against you: 1205
I supplicate you, falling about your chin
And knee and hand,[2] breaking forth into
An old man's tears. Oh, my son,   1210
Check your fierce lion's spirit, by which

---

[1]The plain of Phlegra, the site of the battle of the Giants (see above, n. on 178),
was variously located. Euripides probably thought of it as up north on the
tip of Chalcidice (see map).

[2]On these gestures see above, n. on 987

You are being led to a murderous, impious course,
Wishing to join ills to ills,[1] child.

Theseus
Well now, I tell you, sitting in a sorry state,
To reveal your face to friends;   1215
For no darkness holds so black a cloud
That it could hide your misfortune and ills.
Why, gesturing me away, do you show your fear?
So that the defilement of your greeting may not strike me?
It doesn't matter at all to me if I fare badly along with you.   1220
I fared well with you once. It must be credited to
When you brought me safely into the light from the dead.
I hate friends' gratitude which grows weak with age
And anyone who wishes to benefit from the good things
But *not* to sail with friends in misfortune.   1225
Stand up, unveil your miserable head,
Look at me. Whatever mortal is noble
Bears what falls from the gods,[2] and does not refuse it.

Heracles: *(now unveiled and standing)*
Theseus, do you see this contest of my children?

Theseus
I have heard and you show the ills to my sight.   1230

Heracles
Why then did you uncover my head to the sun?

Theseus
Why? As a mortal you can't stain the things of the gods.

Heracles
Flee, miserable one, my unholy pollution.

Theseus
There is no avenging spirit[3] from friend to friend.

Heracles
Thank you. I don't regret that I helped you.   1235

Theseus
And I, faring well then, pity you now.

Heracles
Am I pitiable after killing my children?

Theseus
I weep for your sake at external misfortunes.

---

[1]Suicide in addition to the murders.
[2]The metaphor, from dicing, is common in Greek literature.
[3]The avenging spirt of the dead which causes pollution.

Heracles
Have you found others in worse ills?

Theseus
You touch heaven from below with your bad fortune.   1240

Heracles
For that reason I'm prepared to die.

[There is probably a lacuna here, most likely of no more than two lines.]

Theseus
Do you think that the gods care at all about your threats?

Heracles
God is stubborn, and I toward the gods.

Theseus
Hold your tongue, so you don't suffer something greater by
     your proud talk.

Heracles
I'm filled with ills and there's no longer a place where they can
     be stowed.   1245

Theseus
But what will you do? Where are you borne in anger?

Heracles
Dying, I will go where I returned from, below the earth.

Theseus
You've spoken the words of a common man.

Heracles
Yes, but you're giving me advice when you're outside
     misfortune.

Theseus
Is it the Heracles who endured many things who says this? 1250

Heracles
Not *so* many. Toiling must have its limit.

Theseus
The benefactor and great friend to mortals?

Heracles
They're no help to me, but Hera holds sway.

Theseus
Greece would not endure your dying through ignorance.

Heracles
Listen now so that I may contend with words against   1255
Your advice. And I will reveal to you

That my life both is unlivable now and was so before.
First of all, I came from this man, the sort who, needing purifica-
     tion
After killing my mother's aged father,[1]
Married Alcmene, who gave me birth.   1260
And whenever the foundation of a family is not laid down
Correctly, it's inevitable that the offspring be unfortunate.
And Zeus, whoever this Zeus is, begot me as an enemy
To Hera (Don't you, old man, be angry:
I consider you, not Zeus, my father),   1265
And when I was still at the breast
The wife of Zeus sent Gorgon-gleaming snakes
Into my cradle so that I might die.[2]
And when I attained the cloak of a vigorous
Body, what need is there to mention the toils I endured?   1270
What sort of lions or three-bodied
Typhons[3] or Giants or war against
Four-legged Centaurs did I not dispatch?
And after killing the dog with heads all around that kept
     growing back,
The hydra, I both went through herds   1275
Of thousands of other labors and arrived among the dead
To convey Hades' three-headed watch-dog
Into the light at Eurystheus' orders.
And this final labor I, the sufferer, endured,
Coping the house with ills by killing my children.   1280
And I have come to this point of necessity: It is not religiously
     permitted
For me to inhabit my dear Thebes. And even if I do remain,
Into what sort of temple or gathering of friends
Shall I go? For the ruin I have forbids my being addressed.[4]
But am I to go to Argos? How, when I'm fleeing my
     fatherland?   1285
But come now, am I to set off for another city?
And then to be looked at askance when recognized,

---

[1]See above, n. on 17.

[2] Even as an infant Heracles was impressively strong: he strangled the snakes.

[3]In Hesiod's *Theogony* Typhon has a hundred heads, all snakes, but such
     numbers were not always immutable. The plural for Typhons here and
     Giants and Centaurs below suggests the host of Heracles' many labors. For
     the Giants and Centaurs see above, n. on 178 and 181.

[4]See above, n. on 1155.

Locked up by bitter and sharp tongues:[1]
"Isn't this Zeus' son, who at one time killed his children
And wife? Let him get the hell out of this land."   1290
[For a man once called blessed
Reversals are something bitter; but the one for whom things
    always
Go badly, since he's innately unfortunate, feels no pain.]
To this point of misfortune I think I'll one day come:
The earth will cry out forbidding me   1295
To touch the land, and the sea and the rivers'
Streams to travel across them, and I'll be just like
Ixion, driven round chained to a wheel.[2]
[And this is the best—for none of the Greeks,
Among whom we were blessedly successful, to look at me.] 1300
Why then should I live? What gain shall I have
In possession of a worthless, unholy life?
Let the famous wife of Zeus dance,
Striking Olympus'[3] sparkling floor with her shoes.
For she has achieved the purpose she wished,   1305
Turning upside down the first man of Greece
From the foundations. Who would pray
To such a goddess? One who because of a woman,
In jealousy over Zeus' union, destroyed
Greece's benefactor, who was not at all blameworthy.   1310

Chorus

This contest is from none other of the gods
Than Zeus' wife. You perceive this well.

Theseus

*[There is a gap of at least one and perhaps of several lines at this point, which
causes a break in the opening of the speech.]*

I would advise you...rather than suffer ills.
But no one of mortals is untouched by fortune
Nor of the gods, if, as I assume, the stories of poets aren't
    false.   1315
Have they not joined in illicit unions
With one another? Have they not defiled their fathers

---

[1]The image, as R. Renehan suggests, is of a tongue having a door and Heracles
being locked up, because in exile he would not able to respond to these
taunts.

[2]Ixion, the first murderer in Greek mythology, was absolved of his crime by
Zeus and repaid the favor by trying to rape Hera. As punishment for this
he was chained to a spinning wheel.

[3]Mount Olympus, the home of the gods.

With bonds for the sake of ruling? But nevertheless they dwell
On Olympus and endure their errors.[1]
And yet what will you say if, a mortal, you   1320
Take these fortunes too much to heart, when the gods do not?
Well, abandon Thebes because of the law
And accompany me to the city of Pallas.[2]
There after I've purified your hands of the pollution[3]
I'll give you a house and a share of my possessions.   1325
And the gifts from the citizens that I have after saving
Fourteen youths by killing the Cnossan bull,[4]
I'll give these to you. And everywhere sections of land
Have been apportioned to me; these will be given your name,
And from now on will be so called by mortals   1330
While you're alive. And whenever you go to Hades,
The entire city of the Athenians will extol you in honor
With sacrifices and memorials of stone.
For it is a fine crown for the citizens to get a good reputation
In the eyes of the Greeks for helping a good man.   1335
And with this favor I will repay you for
Saving me; for now you are in need of friends.
[Whenever the gods give honor, there's no need of friends
For the god helping when he wishes is sufficient.]

Heracles

Oimoi! These things[5] are incidental to my ills;   1340
For I don't believe that the gods put up with
Illicit unions and binding hands with chains—
Neither did I ever think this proper nor will I be persuaded—
Nor that one is by nature master of another.
For god, if he is truly god, lacks   1345
Nothing; these are the wretched stories of poets.[6]

---

[1]The adulterous behavior of Zeus and of other gods was infamous. Binding one's father for the sake of rule refers to Zeus' actions against his father Cronus and Cronus' against his father Uranus. Euripides here and elsewhere (most notably at *Hippolytus* 451ff.) has a character employ an argument based on divine behavior: "If the gods do x and put up with it, shouldn't you also accept x?"

[2]Athens.

[3]The pollution caused by the murder of his family.

[4]Theseus killed the Cnossan (Cretan) Minotaur, a half-man, half-bull creature, and saved the fourteen youths who would otherwise have been offered up to the monster.

[5]"These things" is somewhat vague, but refers to what Theseus has just said, the arguments that Heracles goes on to dispute.

[6]The attack on the gods would have been familiar to some, at least, of the Athenians, since the very same argument was made by the poet-philoso-

But I take care, even in these ills,
That I not, by leaving the light, incur a charge of cowardice.
For anyone who cannot withstand the blows of fortune
Would not be able to withstand a man's weapon.   1350
I will endure life; and I will go to your
City and owe you a thousand thanks for your gifts.
But indeed I tasted a thousand labors,
None of which I refused, nor did I let fall
Streams from my eyes, nor would I ever have thought   1355
That I would come to this —to shed tears from my eyes.
But as things are now, it seems, I must be a slave to fortune.
Well now. Old man, you see my exile
And you see that I'm the murderer of my children.
Give these corpses burial and lay them out,   1360
Honoring them with tears (for me the law does not permit),
Leaning them against their mother's breast, and giving them to
     her embrace,
The wretched partnership that I, the sufferer,
Killed unwillingly. And when you've covered the corpses in the
     earth,
Dwell in this city, even though it will be painful.   1365
[Force your spirit to bear my ills with me.]
Children, I, the father who engendered and begot you,
Killed you, nor did you benefit from my fine things
Which I was preparing, achieving a good reputation
In life for you, a fine advantage from your father.   1370
And you, miserable one, I destroyed, an unequal return
For steadfastly preserving my bed,
Enduring at home long care for the house.
Oimoi for my wife and children, *oimoi* for myself!
How miserably I've fared and have been unyoked   1375
From my children and wife. Mournful joys of
Kisses, and mournful partnership with these weapons.
For I'm at a loss whether I should keep these or abandon them,
Which falling against my sides will say this:
"With us you killed your children and wife; you carry us, 1380
The murderers of your children." Then shall I bear these
In my hands? Saying what? But stripped of the weapons
With which I achieved the finest things in Greece,
Am I to die shamefully, subjecting myself to my enemies?

pher Xenophanes, who lived in the second half of the sixth and into the fifth
century.

These must not be left behind, but be saved, even though
    they pain me.   1385
In one thing, Theseus, work with me: come and
Help me convey the savage dog to Argos,
Lest in grief, bereft of my children, I suffer something.
Land of Cadmus and all Theban people,
Cut your hair,[1] mourn with me, go to the grave   1390
Of the children. And mourn for all of us together,
Both the corpses and me. We are all completely ruined,
Miserable, struck down by one blow of fortune from Hera.

Theseus
Stand up, unfortunate one; enough of tears.[2]

Heracles
I couldn't: my limbs are stiff.   1395

Theseus
Yes, misfortunes overpower even the strong.

Heracles
Oh!
May I be a rock right here, forgetful of ills.

Theseus
Stop. Give a hand to a helping friend.

Heracles
But may I not wipe blood off on your robes.

Theseus
Wipe it off, spare nothing; I don't refuse.   1400

Heracles
Bereaved of my children, I have you as my child.

Theseus
Put your arm on my neck, and I will lead.

(Heracles rises and leans on Theseus for support.)

Heracles
A dear yoking; the other was disastrous.
Old man, one ought to get such a man as a friend.

Amphitryon
The fatherland which begot this one is blessed in its
    children.   1405

---

[1]A sign of mourning.

[2]It seems that Heracles has sunk again to the ground. But it is possible that
he has remained seated among the corpses throughout his conversation
with Theseus.

Heracles
Theseus, turn me around so I may see the children.

Theseus
What for? With this remedy, will you feel better?

Heracles
I desire it, and I wish to embrace my father.

Amphitryon
Look here, child, for you're striving after what's dear to me too.

(They embrace.)

Theseus
Do you thus no longer remember your labors?   1410

Heracles
All those ills I endured are less than these.

Theseus
If someone sees you, he'll not approve your being womanly.

Heracles
In your view, am I to go on living, though humbled? But I don't
   think I did so before.

Theseus
Very much so. In your sickness you are not Heracles the famous.

Heracles
What sort were *you* below, in your ills?   1415

Theseus
In courage I was a man less than everyone.

Heracles
How then do you reproach me that I'm cast down by ills?

Theseus
Go forward.

Heracles
                  Farewell, old man.

Amphitryon
                                    You too, my child.

Heracles
Bury the children, just as I said.

Amphitryon
                                    And who *me*, child?

Heracles
I will.

Amphitryon
> Coming when?

Heracles
> > Whenever you die, father.   1420

[Amphitryon
> How?

Heracles
> I will send for you from Thebes to Athens.]
> But bear the children in, pains that are hard to bear.
> And I, having destroyed my house with shameful deeds,
> All ruined, will follow Theseus, a little boat in tow.[1]
> Whoever wishes to acquire wealth or strength   1425
> More than good friends thinks badly.

(Heracles exits with Theseus down the same parodos from which Theseus first arrived.)

Chorus:[2]
> We go, grieved and much lamenting,
> After losing the greatest of friends.

(The ekkyklema with the corpses is rolled back into the palace and Amphitryon follows it in; the chorus leaves the orchestra via the parodos from which they entered.)

---

[1]On the significance of the unusual word translated "little boat in tow", see *Interpretation*, 84.

[2]The last two lines are in anapestic dimeters, a marching rhythm for the chorus' exit.

The *Heracles*: An Interpretation

About the *Heracles* critical opinion has never been tepid. The verdicts issued both for and against the play have been forceful and some have become almost as famous as their authors. The poet Robert Browning referred to the play as "the perfect piece", while his younger contemporary Swinburne, in a graphic and memorable phrase, called it a "grotesque abortion". The most important classical scholar of the late nineteenth and early twentieth century, Wilamowitz, devoted his masterly study of Greek tragedy to this play, but earlier in this century the influential British classicist Gilbert Murray pronounced it "broken-backed". These critics, and the many others who have shared their views, were responding to the same play, and at times even to the same features of the play. The play is bold in its handling of the myth, ambitious in design, and arresting in its many reversals of fortune. While its supporters have seen it as a superb example of Greek tragedy's potential to delineate the tragic and the humane in life, its critics have been disturbed by its alleged lack of unity, specifically the absence of a clear causal link between the events of the first half of the play and those of the second. Anyone coming to the *Heracles* expecting the tight structure of Sophocles' *Oedipus the King* or Euripides' *Hippolytus* will, doubtless, be disappointed in this regard, but such a narrow notion of unity ill serves a study of Greek tragedy. Every play has its own patterns and rhythm, and a seeming disjuncture may very well be part of its design.

The play's opening suggests to the audience the dire straits of the characters. A group, an old man, a woman, and three young boys, sits at an altar in supplication. The altar, this opening tableau reveals to us, is their only hope of refuge: they are passive and helpless and their leaving the altar will signify their rescue or their doom. The play's first speech, the prologue delivered by Amphitryon, verbally confirms this visual impression of helplessness, as the old man explains that with Heracles away in Hades Lycus has staged a coup in Thebes and now threatens the family of Heracles with death. Amphitryon and the family have accordingly taken refuge at the altar of Zeus the Rescuer, and seek his help since their own true friends are too weak to aid, while others have proven to be not true friends at all. Euripides commonly begins his plays with such an exposition, which not only provides the basic background information to the drama's action but helps to establish the play's themes and mood. Here, for instance, we notice that Amphitryon's opening self-identification (necessary in a theater without playbills) links him with Zeus: "What mortal does not know of the man who shared his marriage bed with Zeus,/Amphitryon of Argos...the father of Heracles? "(1-3). The opening reference to Zeus has double point: it initiates the thematic issue of Heracles' paternity (Is Zeus or Amphitryon his father?) which is developed throughout the play (see, e. g., 1-3, 148-49, 170-71, 339-47, 353-54, 798-804, 1263-65) and it suggests that Zeus, at whose altar these suppliants sit, has special reason to offer them protection, since he has a share in Amphitryon's marriage bed and Heracles' birth.

In providing background information for the play's action, Amphitryon's speech also gives some indication to the audience of the play's assumptions. As discussed in the *Introduction* (12-13), Euripides made several innovations in this play, the most important of which Amphitryon makes clear in this speech: the labors are *not* preceded by the murder of the children. What will happen to them, the audience must wonder? Amphitryon also introduces Lycus and his threat with special care, since he too is new to the tale and is essential for the first half of the action. Not only does Lycus, by threatening the family, motivate the first third of the play, but consequently also allows Heracles to show his deep concern for his family and dispatch the wicked tyrant, all of which leads up to the shocking reversal in the next act.

Amphitryon also announces in his opening speech a theme which proves central to the drama: friendship. The family is in its current plight because, "Some of our friends I realize are not reliable friends,/ While others who truly are cannot help." (55-56) The word translated as friend, *philos*, had, as discussed in the notes (see on 266), a wider range than English "friend": it referred to anyone who was near and dear, including non-family members, as well as those related by blood or marriage. The *philos* whom the family most needs, the one who could readily set things straight, is Heracles, but the first third of the drama assumes that he cannot return from Hades (cf., e. g., 80ff.,145-46, 296-97). Heracles cannot, it seems, save his family, but the dramatic situation demands that he do just that, and this paradox animates the first part of the play.

In her initial response to Amphitryon (60-86), Megara offers a different view of their situation. Whereas Amphitryon explained the general background of their situation, Megara gives a more personal account. In her view her own plight shows the uncertainty of human fortune (62ff.): she has gone from the acme of mortal prosperity to the verge of death. She also paints a vivid picture of the children's anxiety as they expectantly await their father's return. She has abandoned hope, since death, she believes, is inevitable, and she turns to Amphitryon to provide some means of rescue; their safety is in his hands. Amphitryon, by contrast, will not despair: "That man is the best, the one who always/Trusts in hope" (105-06).

At this point the chorus of sympathetic old Theban men arrives in the *orchestra*, just as in Euripides' other so-called "suppliant" plays a chorus concerned with the well-being of the suppliants enters after the opening scene. The identity of the chorus is very well chosen: they are as well-intentioned as they are impotent. Singing their first song, these men of Thebes make clear their infirm condition ("Mere words, the nocturnal semblance/ Of night-time dreams" [112-13], and see 108-110, and 119-130), and their sympathies ("Feeble, but eager still" [114]). At the end of the song they focus on the children and what their loss will mean to Greece, thereby providing a link to the following scene, as immediately after the song they announce the arrival of the man who will cause Greece to lose them, Lycus.

The scene between Lycus and the suppliants is instrumental to the depiction of these characters, to the plot and to the themes of the drama. Attempts to criticize it have been wide of the mark. Lycus offers an unabashed pragmatism: he now holds power (cf. 141-42) and seeks to rid himself of possible avengers for his murder of Megara's father (165-69). To him this is not shamelessness, but prudence (165-66). As for Heracles, Lycus adds his voice to the belief that having gone down to Hades, he cannot return to rescue his suppliant family. And he ridicules the hero's achievements: his reputation rests on exaggerated victories over mere beasts; using the bow, he is a coward, not facing men in battle face to face; the children deserve no special consideration for such deeds of their father. He shows no respect for the altar's sanctuary: when Amphitryon does not yield, but meets and defeats his arguments with his own (170-235), Lycus will resort to force, ordering men to bring wood so he can burn them at the altar (240-46).

Amphitryon tries to maintain his hope. First he launches a long defense of Heracles and his use of the bow. He vindicates Heracles' labors and explains the cleverness of the bow. This latter argument, as has been suggested, may reflect contemporary interest in military strategy, but more importantly, in addition to giving Amphitryon the chance to defeat Lycus in words and proclaim Heracles' bravery, it has a key thematic role in the drama, as the bow is used in the murder of the children and at the end of the play will take on a symbolic value in Heracles' decision to continue with his life. Amphitryon also criticizes Lycus' cowardice, as well as that of Thebes and Greece, for not coming to the family's rescue. He concludes with a feeble threat against Lycus, saying what he would do if he had the strength of his youth (232-35). Like the chorus, he can offer nothing more than words, as Lycus well recognizes (cf. 238-39). Megara, in viewing the situation, displays again her resignation (275-311). She loves her children, of course, but there is no hope of Heracles' return. Death is inevitable and exile, even if offered, would be wretched. Since such is the case, they should seek a death with honor, not burned at the altar, the object of their enemies' ridicule. "Whoever struggles against the fortunes of the gods/ Is eager, but his eagerness is senseless./ For no one will ever make what must happen not happen" (309-11).

The cumulative effect of Lycus' threats and Megara's persuasion succeeds in convincing Amphitryon to abandon the altar. He had wanted to save Heracles' children, but he concludes that he seemed "to desire the impossible" (318; cf. 92). He leaves the altar and offers himself to Lycus; Megara follows and asks only for one favor: to enter the house and dress the children in the adornment of the dead. Lycus agrees and departs, and Megara goes into the house with the children, while Amphitryon remains to address parting words to Zeus. His attack on Zeus seems an appropriate conclusion to this scene. Zeus has proved uncaring ("You were after all less of a friend [philos] than you seemed" [341]) and useless ("But you do not know how to save your friends [philoi]" [346]). His special connection with the family, being "partner in my child" (340), has, Amphitryon concludes, been of no value. These final words of Amphitryon not only highlight the issue of Heracles' paternity but underscore the question of divine justice, which already has been raised (cf. 212). Zeus seems not to care for justice: Heracles' family is going to die.

The chorus' responds to these events by singing of Heracles' labors. They assume he is dead ("Excellent glory achieved with noble toil/ Are glory for the dead" [356-66].) and sing a type of lament (threnos) in his honor. The song has several purposes. First, it offers another response to Lycus' shallow attack on Heracles' heroism. Second, it shows Heracles as a civilizing, beneficial force, subduing the Centaurs who terrorized the Thessalians (364-74), taming the mares of Diomedes who feasted on human flesh (380-86), calming the seas for mortals (400-02). It concludes with the present situation: Heracles is finishing his life in Hades, while the family looks to him in his absence. The chorus cannot help; they lack their "blessed youth". The tension of the play's first section is experienced in miniature in this song: by singing the praises of Heracles, the chorus makes clear how easily he could save his family, while the form of the song, a threnos, reminds us that he is, it appears, dead.

Lycus had said (334-35) that he would return after the family had donned their robes of death. At this juncture, then, we should expect his return, but it is delayed while the pathetic picture of the family, sketched in the previous scene, is painted with full, affecting strokes. Megara turns to the children and describes the games Heracles used to play with them, as he promised them future rule, and she recounts her own choosing of brides for her sons. She concludes with a despairing appeal to Heracles: "Help! Come! Appear to me even as a shadow!" (494). Amphitryon then continues the attack on Zeus which he began at the close of the previous scene, calling upon him, but thinking it a vain appeal. Having been won over to Megara's position, he elaborates on the vicissitudes of life, as seen in his own case; hope he has finally abandoned.

At this moment of despairing resignation to death, Euripides presents the play's first reversal. Heracles is seen approaching. The hero whose return was repeatedly denied as impossible, whose return was the only thing that could save the threatened family, arrives, as if in answer to Megara's appeal, at the critical moment to save his family and punish the tyrant. Euripides exploits the dramatic possibilities of this entrance by drawing it out, displaying Megara's confusion, disbelief and joy. Zeus did not save them, but Heracles will: as Megara explains to the children, to them he is "not at all inferior to Zeus Soter" (522). Shocked at what he sees and angered when he learns the situation and the threat to his family, Heracles vows revenge (565-73). The strong language in which he describes his vengeance has disturbed some critics, leading them to think that Heracles is either already showing signs of incipient madness or that he is guilty of some sort of excess. Neither is the case. Nothing in the play prior to the arrival of Iris and Lyssa suggests his madness (in fact Euripides lays great stress on the madness as sudden and external) and Heracles' threatened vengeance, although it reminds us of the type of violent deeds he is capable of performing, is not out of line with the code of helping your friends and hurting your enemies (cf. note on 266). The prime target of his destruction is the man who threatens his own family and the others are those who tolerated this treatment, when they themselves had benefited from him. The labors have been greatly emphasized in part so Heracles can here disown them in favor of something he values more dearly. "Farewell, labors!" (575). His subduing the Nemean lion and all the other wondrous deeds pale in comparison to his defence of his family. Now his defense of them will become the new test of his heroism (cf. 578-82).

After discussing strategy with Amphitryon, and revealing that he rescued Theseus while he was in Hades (a fact that becomes important later), Heracles calls to his children to enter the house with him. Here we experience visually the reversal presented in this scene, which began with the announced entrance of the children with

Megara and Amphitryon (445-47): "and his loving wife,/ Pulling [*helkousan*] beside her their children/ Who cling to her feet which guide them". Heracles now proclaims, "Taking them [his children who are clinging to his robes] by the hand I will lead these little boats/ And like a ship I will pull [*ephelxo*] them in tow" (631-32). Tears also connect the two stage actions (cf. 449-50, 625). Finally, Heracles himself contrasts their exit from to their entrance into the house: "So your entrances into it are fairer/ Than your exits from it, right?" (623-24). The exit from the house at the beginning of the scene seemed to mark the family's imminent death, but did not, while the entrance into it seems to signal their safety, but this too is only temporary and illusory. Heracles delivers the scene's final words, just as we see what proves to be the last of the children and Megara: "Everyone loves his children" (636).

Heracles' successful return inspires the chorus to sing in celebration (637-700). The previous song was a lamentation over the presumed dead Heracles; this one is a type of victory song, an epinician, praising, indirectly and directly, the living and successful hero. The two songs frame the scene in which the first reversal of fortune, marked by Heracles' return, occurs. Youth, which the chorus has constantly made clear it sorely lacks, is dear to them, old age a burden; wealth, a conventional measure of excellence, is not to be preferred to youth. The gods should give a double youth to those who excel as a clear sign of their excellence. This odd-seeming wish pertains indirectly to Heracles, since having just returned from Hades, he has experienced a type of rebirth and has come to possess symbolically a second youth. Following a common pattern, the first half of this song (the first two stanzas) is general, while the second half is particular, as the chorus turns specifically to their praise of Heracles. They will never stop singing his praises. He is the child of Zeus and is "surpassing/ In excellence (*arete*) more than in noble birth" (696-97).

Once Heracles has arrived, the death of Lycus is a foregone conclusion, and Euripides wastes little time on it. Lycus returns at the start of the next scene, looking for the family he intends to kill. He is tricked, however, by Amphitryon into entering the house, where Heracles lies in ambush (this is an intrigue pattern which Euripides employs elsewhere, e.g. in *Hecuba, Electra, Antiope*). His death screams are interspersed with the chorus' cries of joy at the return of the old ruler and the punishment of the wicked new one. For them this death is proof of divine justice. As they sing in their following song, "The gods, the gods/ Take care to heed/ The unjust and the holy" (772-73). The previous ode not only looked backwards, commenting on the successful return of Heracles and framing with the first stasimon that return, it also with the present song marks the final stage of Heracles' victory, the killing of Lycus. Together these two songs surrounding the brief scene of Lycus' death create an impressive mood of joy and celebration. This change of fortune is proof of a theodicy, and Thebes celebrates with dancing, festival, and song. For the chorus Heracles' success is proof not only of a theodicy but also of his divine birth. Zeus is indeed his father. The serious doubts suggested by Amphitryon's stinging words are forgotten in the joy of this victory. Heracles is Zeus' son and the gods care for justice. The conclusion of the song is confident: "You [Heracles] were a better ruler to me/ Than the ignoble lord,/ Who now, looking on the contest/ Of swords, makes clear/ Whether justice/ Still pleases the gods" (809-14).

At once Iris and Lyssa, the personification of madness, appear on high to madden Heracles into killing his family. The joy of the ode and Heracles' success are short-lived. This juxtaposition of joyous song and destructive action could not be more sudden or arresting. And the appearance of gods in mid-play is unique in Euripides. Elsewhere they appear only at the beginnings and ends of the dramas, and nowhere else do two superhuman characters with speaking parts arrive jointly. This unusual and sudden appearance underscores the reversal which it signals. Iris explains that they mean no harm to the city; only against one man, Heracles, do they come. Ironically Lyssa, the personification of madness, does not wish to madden the intended victim. (Note the similarity between this scene and the opening of *Prometheus Bound*, where another pair of divinities argues about the justice of punishing a mortal who has benefited others and where Hephaestus, the one who ought to be interested in persecuting the mortal, demurs.) She argues (847-54) that Heracles has performed many noble deeds and explains that "he alone restored the honors/Of the gods which fell at the hands of impious men" (852-53). Iris, her superior, demands that she perform her duty and Lyssa does so, forecasting the madness she will bring upon Heracles and his murder of the children.

Why is this madness sent upon Heracles? This question, as much as any other, has disturbed and puzzled critics of the play. Iris gives no long explanation. While Heracles was performing his labors, Necessity and Zeus did not allow Hera or Iris to harm him. Now that he has completed them, they may drive him to kill his children so "he may recognize what sort is Hera's anger against him/ And learn mine. Otherwise the gods are nowhere/ And mortal things will be great, if he doesn't pay the penalty" (840-42). The cause of Hera's anger, unspecified here, is mentioned later in the play (cf. especially 1307-10): Zeus' illicit union with Alcmene and the resulting offspring, Heracles. Even before hearing this expressly, the audience would assume that this is the reason for Hera's anger, since it was well known and already found in Homer's *Iliad* (19. 95ff.). The thematic issue of Heracles' paternity ("Is Zeus or Amphitryon his father?") has, it is seen in this regard, extra point: to keep before the audience's mind the illicit union which produced him. Iris' anger is perhaps somewhat more puzzling. It has been suggested that she acts as a stand-in for Hera in this scene. It would be inappropriate and distracting for the queen of heaven to make such an appearance, and Iris, on a more equal footing with Lyssa, allows for a better contrast between the two opposing characters. She is little more than an alter-Hera and her anger is simply Hera's transferred. In any case, Iris' anger receives little dramatic attention; the focus is on Hera.

Iris' reference to Heracles' "paying the penalty" raises another question: penalty for what? Heracles, many have assumed, must have done something wrong. Various theories have been spun, focusing chiefly on Heracles' alleged *hubris*, his offense of excess, perhaps in coming back from the "dead" in Hades, perhaps by performing his many great deeds. Others have glided over this passage and found the madness in the hero himself, the divine apparatus being a mere symbol of his internal state. Such theories founder, however, on the evidence of the play. Throughout the drama Euripides underscores the external nature of the madness, and nowhere is it suggested that Heracles is guilty of arrogant or excessive behavior. In fact Euripides strives to show the opposite: Heracles has helped the gods in combat (177ff., 1190ff.), restored their honors (852-53), and been a great benefactor to man (cf., especially, the description of the labors in the first stasimon). The gods, however, do not need to satisfy mortal curiosity about the motivation for their actions. From the point of view of Hera (and Iris) Heracles must be "punished", punished for deeds left unspecified. The gods here appropriate language used elsewhere in this play to describe Lycus' punishment (especially in the previous choral celebration, e.g. at 740 and 756). The audience is left to decide whether the divine action conforms to their own notions of justice. Euripides helps them in forming their judgment by offering no evidence of Heracles' "crime" but, on the contrary, much to suggest his piety. The appearance of Iris and Lyssa is meant as a sharp rupture, a sudden and fierce overturning of the previous action. The dramatic rupture underlines the causal one: the drama's action does *not* suggest a reason for Heracles' "punishment" and madness other than the will and power of the gods.

Iris' and Lyssa's appearance occurs roughly at the halfway point of the play and since it so radically changes the play's direction, many have viewed the drama as having two sections, the first consisting of lines 1-814, the second lines 815-end. Others have preferred to see the play as tripartite: the same first part (lines 1-814), a second part

(815-1162), and a third, punctuated by Theseus' arrival, extending from 1163-end. Those who argue for a three-fold division can find support in the surprising entrances of the divinities at 815 and of Theseus at 1163 as signalling the second and third parts respectively. Both sides of the debate are in a way correct. The play does seem to have three divisions, neatly punctuated by the surprise entrances which move the action in new directions (one might argue that Heracles' arrival at 514 constitutes yet another division), yet the actions are fundamentally two, each one of which is then reversed. The first action, the "suppliant" drama is marked by the surprising rescue by Heracles. After this action is completed, the gods arrive, introducing the second action in which Heracles is rescued, and in which several reversals of the first action occur.

We experience Heracles' madness and the murder of his children in several stages. It is first announced by Iris and Lyssa, predicted by the chorus in lyrics, and then followed by Amphitryon's cries from within confirming the bloodshed, interspersed with choral lamentation; a messenger then enters from the palace to narrate the sorry deeds, and finally the corpses and the subdued Heracles are wheeled out on the *ekkyklema* offering visual proof of the events. The messenger's description of the murders is chilling. As Heracles and his family stands around the altar, where he is in the process of performing expiatory sacrifice for his murder of Lycus, the madness struck ("He was no longer himself" [931]). He imagines that he will go after Eurystheus, but in his frenzy he took his own children for those of Eurystheus; the children's rescuer has now become their slayer. In Megara's speech almost immediately before Heracles' return from Hades, she described how the boys' father had given one his club to play with (470ff.), while to another he promised rule over Oechalia, "which he had once sacked with his well-aimed arrows" (473). The messenger relates how with these very weapons he killed his sons and wife (977ff.). The third child is killed as his mother tries to protect him (996-1000), a grim echo of Megara's own words in her first speech (71-72).

Before the carnage is presented visually to the audience, the chorus sings a brief song commenting on the events within. Referring to other examples of kindred murder, the slaying of husbands by the daughters of Danaus and the filicide committed by Procne, they conclude that Heracles' murder of his children surpasses these. The doors then open and the *ekkyklema* reveals the corpses of the three children and Megara and Heracles tied to a broken pillar. This tableau presents a visual echo of the original scene of supplication. The play opened with the children, Megara and Amphitryon gathered around the altar; now we see the corpses of Megara and the children surrounding Heracles tied to a pillar, which, like the altar, is an impressive stage property. The stage now holds two striking reminders of failure. The rescue by Heracles failed, just as the altar of Zeus failed, to protect the family. The now-deserted altar has nearby the scene of divinely-caused slaughter.

Heracles' maddened slaughter was stopped only by the intervention of Athena, who subdued Heracles into sleep by striking him with a rock. Will he be mad when he awakes? Amphitryon's and the chorus' vivid exchange about Heracles and his mental state enlivens the scene. When Heracles does waken, he only gradually realizes what he has done; like Agave in the *Bacchae*, he learns the full horror of his actions in stages. Fully informed of his horrific deeds, Heracles decides on suicide (1146-1152). By this means he will be able "to thrust away my life's infamy which remains" (1152). He describes more fully later (1281ff.) what this infamy will mean. Just as Megara was motivated to abandon the altar by thoughts of the family's reputation (see, e.g., 284-93), Heracles is driven to death by similar considerations. Heracles has now arrived at the point reached first by Megara and then by Amphitryon. He sees no reason for living; he is resigned to death. Like Ajax in Sophocles' play, Heracles is driven to contemplate suicide by the disgrace he feels at his acts. But unlike Ajax, Heracles has someone who will come to save him and help him to live despite his wretched circumstances. No sooner does Heracles finish declaring his plans for suicide than he spots and announces the arrival of Theseus, "interrupting my thoughts of suicide" (1153), whom he describes as his friend (1154, 1156). Ashamed of what he has done and wishing not to pollute Theseus with blood guilt, he covers himself. As mentioned above, the play's three reversals are each marked by a surprise entrance: the arrivals of Heracles, Iris and Lyssa, and now Theseus. We had learned before of Theseus' rescue by Heracles from Hades and his return to Athens (619-21), but we have no reason to expect his arrival here.

This arrival is not only timely in interrupting Heracles' plans of suicide, it also sets in motion the final act of the play. Theseus explains at once that, having learned of political troubles in Thebes, he has come with troops to aid Heracles; he does so in return for Heracles' rescuing him from Hades. The impulse of succor stems from the traditional code of helping friends and harming enemies; this would dictate, as Theseus implies, a return of beneficial action. But Theseus in this scene is depicted as extraordinary. Nothing, not even the threat of pollution, will deter Theseus from befriending Heracles ("But if I come to share the pain? Uncover him" [1202]; "There is no avenging spirit from friend to friend" [1234]). In fact what dominates this final scene is the theme of friendship (cf., e.g., 1154-56, 1169-70, 1200, 1202,

1221-25, 1234, 1336-37, 1403-04). Theseus is adamant in his insistence on helping Heracles. Even at the risk of pollution, even if it means faring poorly (cf. 1220-21), he wants Heracles to unveil himself and to speak with him face to face. He acknowledges that Heracles' ills are great ("For no darkness holds so black a cloud/ That it could hide your misfortune and ills" [1216-17]). But we must endure what comes from the gods ("Whatever mortal is noble/ Bears what falls from the gods, and does not refuse it" [1227-28]). Endurance, especially of what comes from the gods, was a time-honored virtue (cf. especially the example of Odysseus), but Heracles seems to have taken it to a new extreme, one which he feels must have an end: "Toiling must have its limit" (1251). Theseus must not only offer his friendship, but remind Heracles of his heroism: in response to Heracles' threat of suicide, Theseus retorts, "You've spoken the words of a common man" (1248).

The initial exchange between the two men leads to a debate on Heracles' life and suffering, a debate which deserves special attention because it shows how the stricken Heracles, brought from the acme of success to the lowest point of ruin and disgrace, overcomes the blows of fortune, and it also touches on critical thematic issues. Three long speeches form the core of this debate. First Heracles recounts a life of unremitting persecution at the hands of Hera, beginning with the circumstances of his engendering ("Zeus... begot me as an enemy/ To Hera" [1263-64]). The arduous labors culminated in his murder of the children ("This final labor I, the sufferer, endured/Coping the house with ills by killing my children" [1279-80]). Because of the blood pollution, he can no longer live in Thebes. And where else could he turn? What city would receive him? Where would he not be the object of reproach? Even the earth and the sea, he imagines, will cry out that he not touch them. A sufferer since birth, the murderer of his children, cut off from his community in Thebes and any other community, Heracles concludes that his life is not worth living. In his final words he displays his resignation to Hera's power: "Let the famous wife of Zeus dance... For she has achieved the purpose she wished/ Turning upside down the first man of Greece/From the foundations. Who would pray/To such a goddess? One who because of a woman,/ In jealousy over Zeus' union, destroyed/ Greece's benefactor, who was not at all blameworthy" (1303; 1305-10).

Theseus makes a kind of argument not unfamiliar to the audience, an *a fortiori* argument based on divine behavior: the gods err and go on living, will you, a mortal, not do so too? (1314-21) He follows this up with a generous offer of purification of the pollution, a home, gifts, and eventually honorific burial in Athens. All this is repayment for Heracles saving him from the underworld (1336-7). In his initial argument, Theseus with good intentions blurs a distinction between the divine examples and Heracles' situation, a blurring which points to an essential difference. The gods in Theseus' examples deliberately erred and endured, while Heracles has erred unwillingly; he has, in fact, been erred against. Accordingly, in making his comparison Theseus employs the neutral word, fortune (*tuche*), to cover both cases.

The opening of Heracles' reply has generated much discussion, for in these words he raises fundamental questions about divinity and divine justice. To many he seems to be speaking out of character, mouthing the views of the poet himself; but the words have a clear and precise context and are integral to the play, touching upon one of its central concerns. Theseus in his argument had maintained that if, as he assumed, the tales of the poets are true, the gods have engaged in illicit unions and bound their fathers in chains for the sake of rule. Heracles' reply meets his friend's argument point for point, meets it and dismisses its value for his own situation (1340-46):

> *Oimoi.* These things are incidental to my ills;
> For I don't believe that the gods put up with
> Illicit unions and binding hands with chains—
> Neither did I ever think this proper nor will I be persuaded—
> Nor that one is by nature master of another.
> For god, if he is truly god, lacks
> Nothing; these are the wretched stories of poets.

Heracles dismisses Theseus' argument by denying its premise: gods do not behave like that. He does decide to live, but it is because he wishes to avoid the charge of cowardice for taking his own life (1347-48). As he describes it, "For anyone who cannot withstand the blows of fortune/Would not be able to withstand a man's weapon./ I will endure life" (1349-51). He will accept Theseus' gifts and follow him to Athens. Heracles' reply makes clear that his decision to live is based on his own consideration of the cowardice of suicide. His own sense of heroism (*arete*) will not allow him to take his own life. (Contrast, as the original audience must have, the situation of Sophocles' Ajax, whose sense of shame leads him to that very act of self-destruction.) He will even take up the bow, the murder weapon and a harsh reminder of his heinous act, a symbol of his renewed heroism.

The opening of Heracles' reply, although it has a definite context and narrow dramatic purpose, to reply to and to dismiss Theseus' argument, has a larger dramatic function as well. Some critics have tried to make these lines the cornerstone of the play, while others have tried to dismiss them as merely the obtrusive opinion of the poet. Still others, while acknowledging their relevance to the immediate context and debate, deny them any value outside of that context. But in a play in which the question of divine justice and Heracles' paternity are both at issue, it is impossible to deny these lines a significance beyond their immediate context. We have already observed the traditional account of Hera's anger and persecution of Heracles, the account referred to in Heracles' first speech to Theseus (1255-1310), the account assumed and nowhere denied throughout the drama. Heracles' pronouncement on the gods echoes these earlier statements and assumptions. His words also gain a resonance from their clear echo of an earlier poet-philosopher's criticism of the poets' accounts of divine behavior. Writing in the late sixth and early fifth centuries, Xenophanes faulted the poets for wrongly ascribing to the gods rule over one another, adultery, theft, and deception. Heracles, then, is drawing attention to and criticizing the poets (among whom, of course, Euripides is numbered) for their accounts of divine behavior, the type of behavior on which the entire dramatic action, stemming from Zeus' illicit union with Alcmene, is based.

Heracles' words are in opposition not only to what we have heard earlier in the play but also to what Heracles himself says at the end of this speech: "We are all completely ruined / Miserable, struck down by one blow of fortune from Hera" (1392-93). At the end of this speech, which is framed by these statements on divine malfeasance, Heracles returns to the traditional assumptions about the cause of his sufferings and, implicitly, about his paternity. Earlier in this same speech he had said, "I must be a slave to fortune" (1357). Fortune (*tuche*) has not replaced Hera, although that argument has been made. Rather Heracles recognizes that the seemingly random events of his life, culminating in his overthrow at the moment of his greatest victory, have behind them the presence of Hera. She, he concludes, is indeed the cause of his suffering.

But his opening words in this final speech, even if he implicitly rejects them, have a greater significance to the audience. Unlike the character Heracles, who exists only to the extent that the dramatist creates, the audience, and readers of the play, are free to consider and evaluate the implications of Heracles' assertion. And the events of the play provide ample motive for doing so, as the issue of divine justice has been raised from the beginning of the drama. The altar of Zeus the Rescuer, an altar established by Zeus' own son, seems to offer no protection to that son's family and the man whose wife Zeus shared. Amphitryon puts the issue of divine justice into sharp focus in his two "challenging prayers" to Zeus (339ff., 499ff.). And then, when all seems lost, Heracles returns to save the family, proof to the chorus' mind that the gods do care for justice. But the appearance of Iris and Lyssa shatter that belief. That scene serves, in a way, as a counterpart to Heracles' later pronouncement on the gods. The interruption of the two gods is, we have seen, in several ways extraordinary. It emphasizes the external causation of Heracles' madness, laying bare the divine machinery and underscoring the gods' extreme cruelty and injustice, at least when viewed from the human perspective, the perspective of the audience which must interpret these events. In the play's conclusion an irony is thus created as Heracles accepts one notion of divinity and the audience is invited to at least consider another, contradictory one.

Our final impression of Heracles is not of a defeated hero. He has gone through the worst labor (cf. 1279-80) and survived. He has survived not because of the gods (although Athena did intervene to stop him from killing his father) but in spite of them and because of the human friendship provided by Theseus. Theseus offers his aid and comfort as a return on Heracles' initial act of friendship, a point made several times in the drama. The traditional code of helping your friends has served Heracles well. Although Theseus' arrival and succor are crucial to the plot and Heracles' survival, it is Heracles, the play makes clear, who decides on his own beliefs to choose life. Nor is he fundamentally changed. His painful decision to take up the same bow with which he killed his family (1376-85) helps to demonstrate not so much a new, revised heroism (*arete*), as a revived one, one that is able to flourish because of his friendship with Theseus. He is not self-sufficient: he needs his friend Theseus in order to live. The importance of his near and dear ones (*philoi*), which he began to realize in the rescue of his family (see 574ff.) he more fully understands in being rescued by Theseus.

The play ends with separation and departure. Prohibited from burying his family and unable to remain in Thebes, Heracles must leave Amphitryon. This painful parting is drawn out affectingly. Finally Heracles exits with Theseus. He has made the decision to leave, but his reliance on Theseus' friendship is symbolically shown in the final stage action: "And I, having destroyed my house with shameful deeds, / All ruined, will follow Theseus, a little boat in tow" (1423-24). The echo of his earlier words as he led his children into the house (631-32), especially of the very rare word for "little boat in tow" is clear and important. As discussed above, the exit of the family with Heracles into the house echoed their earlier entrance from it. Now this final exit echoes the earlier one. These three actions, each articulating an important stage of the action, suggest in outline the play's progression. In the first, the former suppliants enter to seemingly certain death, but they are rescued and then exit to apparent safety, where in fact they will be fiercely murdered. The final exit, mirroring the first, provides true safety, as Heracles departs to haven in Athens.

Heracles' closing words continue the theme of friendship: "Whoever wishes to acquire wealth or strength / More than good friends, thinks badly" (1425-26). And the chorus has the play's final words, also on this theme: "We go, grieved and much lamenting,/ After losing the greatest of friends" (1427-28). The importance of friendship was announced first in the conclusion of Amphitryon's opening speech and has been repeated throughout the drama. Friendship remains even when all else seems inconstant. Heracles does not defeat the gods, nor does he better Hera. The play suggests the power of the gods, even while suggesting that our comprehension of them might be faulty. The vicissitudes of life, the role of fortune (not Fortune) are nowhere more forcefully seen than in this view of Heracles' life. At the moment of his greatest success, rescuing his family, which he has declared more important than his just-completed labors, Heracles suffers a complete reversal of fortune. He becomes not his family's rescuer, but their murderer. Even the greatest hero is subject to the cruellest and most terrible ruin. The Greeks, from the time of Homer onward, understood that success was ephemeral, but the turnabout here is as shocking and total as anything in Greek literature. And, as we have seen, Euripides has tailored the traditional version of the myth in order to emphasize this point. The juxtaposition of the two actions is his design, not his failing. Although Heracles cannot control all the elements of his life, he can make some decisions within it. Buoyed by the friendship of Theseus, he is able to reject suicide and go on living. According to Greek myths, Heracles eventually became a full-fledged deity, a reward for his labors and suffering. Euripides avoids any mention of and even any allusion to this later apotheosis in order to focus on the human Heracles, a Heracles who, sustained by human friendship, can survive in a capricious and harsh world.

Suggested Further Readings

[The critical writing on Greek tragedy, the ancient theater, Euripides and the Heracles, is vast. What follows is a short list of some works which are accessible and informative. It should not be taken as a comprehensive guide to the scholarship on these topics.]

1. The Theater and Production

J. Gould "Tragedy in Performance" in *The Cambridge History of Classical Literature*, vol. 1 *Greek Literature*, eds. P. Easterling and B. Knox (Cambridge 1985) 263-81. [concise treatment of the major issues]

Pickard-Cambridge, A. W. *The Dramatic Festivals of Athens* 2nd ed., rev. by J. Gould and D. M. Lewis, (Oxford 1968). [comprehensive and scholarly]

Pickard-Cambridge, A. W. *The Theatre of Dionysus in Athens* (Oxford 1946). [comprehensive and scholarly]

Taplin, O. *Greek Tragedy in Action* (Berkeley and Los Angeles 1978). [excellent introduction to the subject]

86

2. Euripides' Life and his Times

Ehrenberg, V. *From Solon to Socrates*, 2nd ed. (London 1973). [history of the sixth and fifth centuries]

Lefkowitz, M. *The Lives of the Greek Poets* (Baltimore 1981). [study of the ancient biographies, including translations of the lives]

Stevens, P. T. "Euripides and the Athenians," *Journal of Hellenic Studies* 76 (1956) 87-94.

The World of Athens: An Introduction to Classical Athenian Culture Joint Association of Classical Teachers (Cambridge 1984).

3. General Works on Euripides and on Greek Tragedy *[those marked with an asterisk include a study of the Heracles]*

Barlow, S. *The Imagery of Euripides*, 2nd ed. (London 1986).

Burnett, A. P. *Catastrophe Survived: Euripides' Plays of Mixed Reversal* (Oxford 1971)*.

Collard, C. *Euripides* Greece & Rome New Surveys in the Classics (Oxford 1981).

Conacher, D. *Euripidean Drama: Myth, Theme and Structure* (Toronto 1967)*.

Foley, H. *Ritual Irony: Poetry and Sacrifice in Euripides* (Ithaca 1985)*.

Halleran, M. *Stagecraft in Euripides* (London and Sydney 1985)*.

Jones, J. *On Aristotle and Greek Tragedy* (Oxford 1962).

Kitto, H. D. F. *Greek Tragedy*, 3rd ed. (London 1961)*.

Lesky, A. *Greek Tragic Poetry*, trans. M. Dillon (New Haven 1983).*
  [thorough survey of the three tragedians]

Murray, G. *Euripides and His Age*, 2nd ed., (New York and London 1946).

Webster, T. B. L. *The Tragedies of Euripides* (London 1967). [particularly good on the "fragmentary" plays]

4. Studies of the *Heracles*

Arrowsmith, W. "Introduction to *Heracles*" in *The Complete Greek Tragedies*, eds. D. Grene and R. Lattimore, Euripides, Vol. 2 (Chicago 1956).

Adkins, A. W. H. "Basic Greek Values in Euripides' *Hecuba* and *Hercules Furens*," *Classical Quarterly* new series 16 (1966) 193-209.

Barlow. S. "Structure and Dramatic Realism in Euripides' *Heracles, Greece & Rome* 29 (982) 115-25.

Chalk, H. "*Arete* and *bia* in Euripides' *Herakles*," *Journal of Hellenic Studies* 82 (1962) 7-18.

Furley, D. "Euripides on the Sanity of Herakles" in *Studies in Honour of T. B. L. Webster*, vol. 1, eds. J. H. Betts, J. T. Hooker, J. R. Green (Bristol 1986) 102-113.

Gregory, J. "Euripides' *Heracles*," *Yale Classical Studies* 25 (1977) 259-75.

Halleran, M. "Rhetoric, Irony and the Ending of Euripides' Herakles," *Classical Antiquity* 5 (1986) 171-181.

Kamerbeek, J. C. "Unity and Meaning of Euripides' *Heracles*," *Mnemosyne* 19 (1966) 1-16.

Lee, K. "The Iris-Lyssa Scene in Euripides' *Heracles*," *Antichthon* 16 (1982) 44-53.

Shelton, J. "Structural Unity and the Meaning of Euripides' *Herakles*," *Eranos* 77 (1979) 101-10.